RISE UP MY LOVE, AND COME AWAY

A Study on Spiritual Growth from the

Song of Solomon

GEORGENE SHALM

RISE UP, MY LOVE, AND COME AWAY

A Study on Spiritual Growth from the Song of Solomon

GEORGENE SHALM

All scripture quotations are taken from the King James Version of the Bible (KJV) unless otherwise noted.

Cover Design by Melissa Baker-Nguyen

Typesetting by Michael. F. Blume

INTRODUCTION

One day several years ago I found myself digging into the Old Testament book, The Song of Solomon. Anyone who's tried to read and study this little gem will agree that it's confusing, mystical, and mystifying. Once in a while, the author comes up for air and writes a few lines that seem clear-cut: the little foxes spoiling the vine is one example, jealousy being as cruel as the grave is another. It seemed as I read, though, that layers of symbolic and poetic language were peeled back, and the Lord gave me an understanding of the deeper meaning of this passionate book.

The very first verse of the Song of Solomon states, "The Song of Songs, which is Solomon's." In other words, Solomon wrote many, many songs, but this one is his masterpiece. I'd have to say that, if the Biblical Song of Solomon is anything to go by, the rest of his songs must have been almost unintelligible! This one is definitely not easy to understand, particularly since the poetic language of the East is very different from the way we speak today.

As I studied various internet sites about the Song of Solomon, I learned that many scholars and theologians feel that it was included in the Bible by mistake; that it is merely a sample of Jewish poetry, very sensual, but of little spiritual value. There were a few scholars who suggested that the Song of Solomon is a drama, written in Oriental poetic language, full of mystical images and word pictures that describe the developing relationship between a young man and an unsuitable girl he has fallen in love with. But very, very few that I studied went so far as to say it was a poetic, prophetic picture of the Lord Jesus Christ and His bride.

I would like to suggest to you that the Song of Solomon was the original "Pilgrim's Progress." Pilgrim's Progress was an allegorical book written by John Bunyan in the 1600s, and is the story of a pilgrim navigating the various stages of life on his way to Heaven. The Song of Solomon is also allegorical and metaphorical, often using unusual word pictures that we in our modern setting don't relate to, to describe qualities and attributes of the characters, and to draw a picture for us of the spiritual journey of a believer from the first moments of feeling convicted for their sin to a level of walking with the Lord in confidence and maturity.

Ultimately, I believe, the beauty of the Song of Solomon is that it is a picturesque description of Jesus falling in love with you and me, and in turn, of you and me falling in love with Jesus. And from that point, we can follow the pathway of every believer as they grow into maturity in this spiritual journey.

The Song of Solomon is not a book about salvation. It is a book about *relationship;* our relationship with the Bridegroom and the Lover of our Souls. It is a textbook for those of us who long to be intimate with our Saviour. It is a love story, describing the romance of our walk with the Lord from our initial experience of salvation to the final day when we are either caught up to meet Him in the air or we pass through the thin veil of flesh to be present with the Lord. Through this age-old story, we will see and understand the various stages of our relationship with Jesus, from the entry level of a brand-new convert, to the final stage of a stable, mature believer. You will notice that the themes of growth, gardens and fruitfulness are often repeated throughout the writing, because we're being invited to grow spiritually, to put down deep roots in the Word, and to be productive followers of our Lover and Bridegroom, the Lord Jesus Christ.

In this personal study of the Song of Solomon, I have chosen to follow the pattern of a play that could be performed on a stage, with various acting and speaking parts and a changing backdrop. But before the curtain opens, let me explain a few things that will clarify the setting for this amazing love story.

The first hint of the plot is given in the final verses of the closing chapter. Chapter 8:11-12 says, "Solomon had a vineyard at Baal-hamon: he let out the vineyard unto keepers, every one for the fruit thereof was to bring a thousand pieces of silver. My vineyard, which is mine, is before me."

King Solomon owned a piece of property in an actual place called Baal-hamon. He leased the property out to labourers who used it as an orchard and a vineyard.

Apparently, the King wanted to check up on the folks who were leasing his land. He knew if he showed up in his kingly vestments they would put on a show for him, and he wouldn't be able to observe them in their regular routines and day-to-day activities. He decided to disguise himself as a shepherd. No one working in the field would recognise the shepherd standing on the edge of the vineyard as the King.

Shortly after King Solomon, dressed as a shepherd, arrived on the scene, his eye was drawn to a beautiful young woman who was one of the peasant labourers. In her present condition at that moment, she would have never been a candidate to be invited to His royal court. But King Solomon couldn't take his eyes off her, and once he caught her eye their passionate courtship began. It was "love at first sight" for both of them. Step by step, incident by incident, we follow the progress of their love story from the thrilling infatuation at the beginning to their deep, mature love in the final chapter.

In this drama, the pursuer and the pursued take turns speaking, relating their love story and its progress. The glitch for us readers is that it's not always clear who's speaking when, and to whom. I have taken the liberty to make decisions regarding the speaker whenever the identity is not clear.

Because the story revolves around a man and his chosen bride, I have used feminine pronouns when referring to her. The Bride of Christ, however, is made up of men, women and children, so the fulfilment of this little book applies to all of us, whether male or female.

Table of Contents

Rise up, My Love, And Come Away

ACT I

Act I, Scene I
The Beginning of the Relationship
(New Believer)
Song of Solomon 1:2-8

2 Let him kiss me with the kisses of his mouth: for thy love is better than wine.

The curtain opens with a flourish on this first scene of King Solomon's drama. The audience sees a beautiful young woman standing on the stage, dressed in the simple clothing of a peasant, her arms flung wide and an expression of ecstasy on her face. The backdrop behind her shows rows of ripening grapevines. It's very obvious to those in the audience that she's not particularly interested in those vines at this moment, though, because her attention is focused on a man in shepherd's attire who stands in the shadows, slightly off stage.

Her opening words, spoken in a rapturous voice are, "Let him kiss me with the kisses of his mouth: for your love is better than wine." Well, that's quite a beginning, I would say! This kiss, my friends, is not a friendly peck on the cheek, but rather an intimate, *passionate* kiss with a hunger for more intimacy to come. We are being invited to observe a brand new, gloriously exciting relationship between a simple maiden and a handsome shepherd.

The young woman is a labourer in a vineyard, and has probably tasted some of the best wine that was produced there. In her limited world and experience, wine is the only commodity to which she can compare this new experience of falling in love, and she declares that this feeling is better than any wine she has ever tasted!

This opening scene is a poignant picture of a brand-new Believer, very recently delivered from a life of sin. This is *you and me* as we stood or knelt at an altar of repentance the first time, and felt the load of sin roll off our shoulders. The new Believer has no idea of the future journey she will take with this handsome stranger who has walked into her life. In this moment she is only concerned with one thing: the passion of this brand-new love.

The besotted maiden represents a "new creature" who has fallen in love with Jesus, even though he or she doesn't really know much about Him. She is now one who loves the presence of the Lord, loves to worship, loves being in and around the altar, loves serving at the pot-luck dinner, loves everything about the church. Can't get enough of Jesus. Oh my, such wonderful days filled with passion, joy and peace! There is nothing this new Believer can think of from her past life which even remotely compares to the love she is feeling in this present moment. Your love is better than wine, she declares. My worst day as a born-again believer is better than my best day was as a sinner!

*3 Because of the savour of thy good ointments thy
name is as ointment poured forth.*

One of the first reactions any new Believer has as they fall in love with Jesus, is to begin to love His Name. That beautiful, miraculous Name of Jesus! How often I have spoken that Name over my restless babies, raging with fever, or beside the bedside of a dear friend suffering in pain. Jesus. Jesus. *Jesus*! There is no other name that compares to His precious Name.

We all come to Jesus with various wounds and bruises. Life hasn't always treated us kindly. As we enter His presence, the ointment of His Spirit is administered to those wounds and the healing process begins. Normally we would expect the medicinal ointment to sting. But *this* ointment is different: the savour is pleasant and the pain of the wounds is soothed.

I am intrigued by the words "poured forth." Not a little dab of ointment spread over an open wound; this ointment is in plentiful supply and can be applied lavishly and generously to our broken spirits and our broken hearts. How often have we, as children, been instructed to "just take a little bit…?" The opportunity to be immersed in healing oil, to be covered from head to toe, to not have to worry about leaving some for the next person in line is awesome! The ointment has been *poured forth*! It's available to one and all, without limitations. The words abundance and limitless come to mind as I think about His Name being poured forth into the world. My mind sees a picture of a fathomless ocean instead of a little pond. Whatever you need from

Jesus, however deep the wounds or the pain, there is always more than enough ointment for you.

Savour is defined as the quality in a substance that is perceived by the sense of taste or smell.

In Exodus 30:23-25, God gave Moses a recipe for the anointing oil that was to be used in the Tabernacle. Into five hundred shekels of pure myrrh (12.5 pounds or 5.5 kilograms), Moses was instructed to mix two hundred and fifty shekels of sweet cinnamon and the same amount of sweet calamus. Five hundred shekels of cassia, and an hin of olive oil (1.5 gallons or just over 5.5 litres) were to be added and then all the ingredients would be stirred together. The result was a unique oil like none other. I'm quite familiar with the delicious aroma of cinnamon, but not so much the other ingredients. However, I'm sure that this anointing oil had a very distinctive scent that would not be confused with any other type of oil. It had a very special and totally unique identifying "savour."

Jesus is the anointed One who was "poured forth" on Calvary for our sins. In Luke 4:18, a verse we will come back to again later, Jesus declared, quoting from the prophet Isaiah, that "the Spirit of the Lord is upon me, because he has *anointed* me to preach the gospel to the poor; he has sent me to heal the broken-hearted, to preach deliverance to the captives, and recovering of sight to the blind, to set at liberty them that are bruised." How thankful we are that His precious Name has been poured into our lives! The Name of Jesus has been poured out, and is all over every aspect of our spiritual experience, from repentance at the altar, to baptism at the laver, to the Holy Place, where we are filled with His Spirit. Jesus, oh how sweet the Name! The pleasing aroma of His precious Name and the healing qualities of the oil of the Holy Ghost that is poured into our wounded spirits has no equal in the world.

After the initial experience of repentance at the altar, the next step all new Believers need to take is into the waters of baptism, where the Name of Jesus is applied and all sin he or she has ever committed is washed away. And finally, Jesus declared in John 14:26 that the Father would send the Comforter, the Holy Spirit in His Name.

In all the steps of our salvation experience, according to Peter's declaration in Acts 2:38, His Name is as ointment poured forth, forgiving us, remitting our sins, healing our broken bodies and spirits and filling us with the powerful Holy Ghost.

Where would we be without that wonderful Name of Jesus?

> *4 Draw me, we will run after thee: the king hath brought me into his chambers: we will be glad and rejoice in thee, we will remember thy love more than wine: the upright love thee.*

Verse 4 of this first chapter has five individual phrases in it that are spoken by two different voices.

The New Believer says, "Draw me," and several of her friends from the vineyard join in by saying, "We will run after thee." Apparently, there was more than one who was attracted to this interesting stranger. However, as the story progresses, we discover that not all of them actually pursued this experience. They had the best of intentions at the outset, but before long most of them had fallen back and only our New Believer/Bride followed on to know the Lord, as Hosea stated, "Then shall we know, if we follow on to know the Lord" (Hosea 6:3). These "others" show up at various points to express opinions or to ask challenging questions, but none of them make the decision to actually "run after thee."

The Bride then makes a statement of fact: The King has brought me into his chambers. I now belong to him. As she speaks, she is looking back after a series of amazing experiences and revelations, to the beginnings of their loving relationship. She certainly didn't know He was the King when she first fell in love with the shepherd standing at the perimeter of the vineyard!

Her "friends" then congratulate her, telling her how happy they are for this exciting new experience she's having. *We'll never forget watching the two of you as you were drawn to each other; your ecstasy was more than those times when we all enjoyed the best of our vineyard's wine together!* We've decided not to come with you, but we're going to be watching you to see what happens next!

And finally, the New Believer/Bride turns to her Lover with an understanding expression on her face. "I get it," she says. "I'd expect that everyone would want to have the same experience as I've had.

But apparently that's not the case. However, there *are* those individuals who have hungry hearts, who are the *upright*, and they are the ones who will persevere in their pursuit of growing and knowing the Shepherd/King." I plan to be one of that small minority. I don't want to be just an observer standing on the fringes, watching someone else growing into a deep relationship; I want to know you myself, personally and intimately.

Now begins the recounting of this amazing, loving and growing relationship that will continue for eight chapters, with the maiden, the new Believer, being brutally honest as she relates the ups and downs of her spiritual experience. She takes us with her, step-by-step from her first encounter with the Shepherd, as she learns about His grace, His mercy, His patience, His plan and purpose for her life to the point where she is His well-beloved and trusted Bride. Each one of us, as believers, will be able to relate to the stages she goes through on her journey with the Shepherd who has stolen her heart.

*5 I am black, but comely, O ye daughters of Jerusalem,
as the tents of Kedar, as the curtains of Solomon.*

Almost immediately the maiden senses a marked difference between herself and the young man who is standing at the edge of the vineyard, trying to catch her eye. "*I am black,*" she says. I am sunburned from being out in the field. I am unworthy of this stranger's attention. The results of my sinful lifestyle have blackened my heart.

A scholar many centuries later penned the same sentiment, "For I know that in me (that is, in my flesh,) dwelleth no good thing" (Romans 7:18).

But wait! The realisation slowly dawns that this handsome stranger, for some reason, finds her, a simple, sunburned maiden, attractive. His loving glance in her direction makes the maiden aware of that fact. With a slight shrug of surprise, she goes on to say, *"but comely,"* because apparently, *He* thinks she is beautiful! He sees value in her that no one else has ever seen. The Shepherd's perspective of this sun-burned peasant girl is very different from her own perspective of herself. She sees all the faults; He sees all the potential.

At this juncture, a very interesting comparison is made by the maiden: on one hand, she feels like the tents of Kedar, and on the other hand, the curtains of Solomon.

The 'tents of Kedar' is a reference to the nomadic, Arabic tribes of northern Africa. Not only were they dark-skinned because of the effect of the relentless desert sun, but their tents were made from the woven hair of black goats. The Kedarites dwelled in the wilderness, an isolated, barren existence. The curtains of Solomon, on the other hand, were hung in the palace, an abode where luxury was the norm. The palace curtains were woven of the finest materials available, probably embroidered with gold and silver threads.

The brand-new Believer is saying to us, I AM NOT WHAT I USED TO BE! Nor am I yet what I will be! But this is my story: I felt convicted of my sin. I knew I was unworthy of the love of this handsome Shepherd. My heart was black with sin. But that's not me anymore! I have been born again. My life has been changed. I have transitioned from a goats' hair tent in the wilderness to the palace of the King. Paul the Apostle put it this way in Colossians 1:14-15, "Who hath delivered us from the power of darkness, and hath translated us into the kingdom of his dear Son: In whom we have redemption through his blood, even the forgiveness of sins."

> 6 Look not upon me, because I am black, because the sun hath looked upon me: my mother's children were angry with me; they made me the keeper of the vineyards; but mine own vineyards have I not kept.

The new Believer reiterates the shame she felt when she sensed the Shepherd's eyes upon her. His presence at the vineyard has convicted her. She explains that she hasn't been able to take care of her own spiritual life because someone else has been directing her actions, causing her to do things she wouldn't necessarily choose to do. Again, the Apostle Paul said it best in Romans 7:18-19, "For to will is present with me; but how to perform that which is good I find not. For the good that I would I do not: but the evil which I would not, that I do." The New Living Translation says it like this, "And I know that nothing good lives in me, that is, in my sinful nature. I want to do what is right, but I can't. I want to do what is good, but I don't. I don't want to do what is wrong, but I do it anyway." This is the condition so many of us found ourselves in before being filled with the transforming power of the Holy Spirit: despite our good intentions, we found ourselves yielding to the temptation of sin, seemingly helpless to make better choices.

7 Tell me, O thou whom my soul loveth, where thou feedest, where thou makest thy flock to rest at noon.

Because she doesn't know His true identity, the new Believer and future Bride assumes that this young man who is attracted to her is a shepherd from out of town. To begin the conversation she asks him, "Where do you feed your flock and where do you make them rest?"

When we first meet Jesus, we are enraptured by His presence. As "new babes in Christ" who are *spiritually immature*, we want to *feel,* we want to be *blessed,* we want to be *fed,* we want to be *taken care of.*

At this time of making the Shepherd's acquaintance the future Bride's main concern is *nourishment* and *rest.* If you asked her, she would say, "I'm hungry and I'm tired. The world hasn't been kind to me. I've been labouring in the vineyard. I need some tender, loving care. I'm like a newborn! I can't do anything for myself." Every pastor knows how demanding new converts can be. They don't hesitate to call at midnight if they are struggling with temptation.

Oh, but didn't Jesus say, "Suffer the little children to come unto me"? Didn't He say, "Blessed are they who do hunger and thirst after righteousness"? Didn't He say, "Come unto me all ye that labor and are heavy laden and I will give thee rest"? Oh, yes! That's exactly what Jesus said, because He totally understands us and our need for rest, sustenance and validation.

Although we might initially interpret these questions as childish and selfish, they are actually a clear depiction of the mindset of a new Believer, excited to be involved with Jesus, but lacking the spiritual resources to meet even the most basic spiritual needs.

Although such a mindset is the norm for a *new* believer, it's important that we don't get stuck at this initial stage. Someone who always needs to be blessed, always has needs to be met, is always being lulled to sleep, is clearly spiritually immature. It's essential that we continue to grow and develop into a mature relationship with Jesus.

8 If thou know not, O thou fairest among women, go thy way forth by the footsteps of the flock, and feed thy kids beside the shepherds' tents.

The Shepherd, who has been standing in the shadows at the side of the stage all this time, now responds to the question posed by the young woman who has caught his eye.

This is the first time we hear His voice. There is not a trace of condemnation in His words. He doesn't berate her for her lack of knowledge. He doesn't condemn her for being self-absorbed. Instead, He simply and gently advises, If you don't know the way, follow the flock to the shepherds' tents. There are others who *do* know the way, just follow their lead. Oh, the wonderful benefit of having Godly examples! And what a great responsibility has been put upon those of us who have known the Lord for some time, to lead others in The Way.

There is great significance in the King being disguised as a shepherd in this opening scene! David wrote, "The Lord is my shepherd, I shall not want" (Psalms 23:1). Isaiah prophesied, "He shall feed his flock like a shepherd, he shall gather the lambs with his arm, and carry them in his bosom, and shall gently lead those that are with young" (Isaiah 40:11). Jesus told his disciples, "I am the Good Shepherd" (John 10:11). When we first become acquainted with Jesus, His role in our life is one of caring for us, feeding us, patching up our wounds, guiding us to verdant pastures. Later on in our walk with the Lord we will understand His majesty, authority and power, but at the beginning of this Godly adventure, we say with David, Yes, the Lord is *my* shepherd.

However, we will soon learn that the Shepherd's intention is not for us to stay in this condition of always being taken care of. His intention is to take us on an amazing journey of discovery where we become strong, knowledgeable, responsible and productive citizens of His Kingdom.

End of Act I, Scene I

Act I, Scene II
The Introduction to Worship
(New Believer)
Song of Solomon 1:12

12 While the king sitteth at his table, my spikenard sendeth forth the smell thereof.

In this statement the new Believer reveals that a gradual change has been taking place in her understanding. Whereas previously, when we first made her acquaintance, her only concern was being fed and taken care of by the *shepherd*, she now recognises, perhaps subconsciously, that there is a *kingly* aspect to Him. She sees Him in a different role, seated at a table. This is not a table spread with food to meet her needs, but one from which business is conducted and directions are given. Here we see a brief glimpse of His authority which she will comprehend more fully later on.

As time has elapsed, the maiden's response to the Shepherd has changed. Their relationship is moving to a different level. No longer focused solely on her needs being met, she has stepped into an atmosphere of worship: *"My spikenard sends forth the smell thereof."*

Spikenard, a perfumed oil, came from the Himalaya mountainous areas of India, present-day Pakistan and Nepal, a great distance from the setting of this dramatic song. Its journey to this location would have been on very dangerous highways and byways. The possibility of thieves intercepting the caravan and stealing the goods was high. Much time was taken getting to the final destination. Dust storms, pouring rain, landslides, accidents and sickness and other emergency situations all had to be faced on the way. Therefore, its inaccessibility made spikenard rare, precious and very expensive. Spikenard became a symbol of worship that had an expensive price tag for the worshipper. The new Believer qualifies it as *my* spikenard. Not corporate, but very personal. *My* worship. *My* relationship with Jesus.

Many centuries later, John wrote about an incident in the life of Jesus that occurred just a few days before His crucifixion, when Mary, the sister of Lazarus, anointed Jesus' feet with very costly spikenard, and wiped them with her hair. "Then took Mary a pound of ointment of spikenard, very costly, and anointed the feet of Jesus, and wiped his feet with her hair: and the house was filled with the odour of the ointment...Then said Jesus, Let her alone: against the day of my burying has she kept this" (John 12:3,7). Several onlookers were disturbed at the waste of such expensive ointment. Jesus, however, recognised what Mary did as an act of deep worship. In a few days' time, Jesus would be transitioning from the humble itinerant teacher walking the dusty Galilean roads to the King of Kings, seated at the right hand of the throne of God in Heaven. The aroma of Mary's costly spikenard ointment accompanied Jesus during his final days, up to and perhaps even during his excruciating crucifixion. At that crucial moment in history, echoes of another worshipper could be heard,

"While the king sits at his table, my spikenard sends forth the smell thereof."

True worship is not cheap or easy. Bouncing on your toes and clapping your hands to a catchy rhythm doesn't cost much except a small amount of energy and a few calories. However, after you have walked through some of life's darkest and most painful valleys where your heart has been broken and your dreams have been shattered, you will learn that being able to stand with your arms raised to Heaven, a song of praise on your lips and salty tears on your cheeks is very, very expensive. It literally costs you everything you have. That kind of worship never comes at a half-price discount. It's not the Dollar Store variety. That kind of worship is the unparalleled perfume of precious, rare spikenard being poured out from your broken alabaster box.

End of Act I, Scene II

Act I, Scene III
The Beginning of Intimacy
(New Believer)
Song of Solomon 1:13

13 A bundle of myrrh is my wellbeloved unto me; he shall lie all night between my breasts.

Our main character, the new Believer/Bride is progressing from someone who is in a constant state of neediness to someone who can give love as well as receive it. She is no longer alone on the stage but has been joined by the One who has fallen in love with her. The marriage ceremony has not been shared with us in any detail, except for the reference early in the first scene of the drama where the Bride states that "the king hath brought me into his chambers," however, it's clear that the peasant, undeserving maiden has by now become the Shepherd's bride, and has left her labour in the vineyard far behind. In this scene, they unashamedly embrace intimately. The Shepherd/King has wooed her and her fears of being unworthy of His love have been dispelled. She calls Him her "wellbeloved". Their words of love to each other reveal that the new Believer is no longer merely infatuated by an emotional sensation. She has fallen deeply in love with a person and has joined her life to his, leaving behind all the experiences of her past.

How sad that these ancient words of love have been twisted by modern theologians and religious scholars into something that is only sexual. There is so much depth and significance to these verses!

At the time Solomon was writing his poetry, myrrh was very expensive and precious. It had a pleasant aroma but was bitter if ingested. The word *myrrh* originated in the Arabic language and means "bitter". Myrrh was the first and main ingredient in the oil used to anoint the tabernacle in the wilderness, all its furnishings, and the priests who would minister therein, which was an indication of the cost exacted from those in ministry, even until today. Myrrh was one of the gifts brought to Jesus by the wise men after his birth. The gift of myrrh to the newborn King was a prophetic foreshadowing of the bitter suffering He would endure at Calvary. In this passage, the young lady is revealing to us that she esteems this new relationship as something very precious and intimate. She is learning that it could involve suffering. She could be required to take up her own cross and bear it courageously. There could be severe trials of her faith in her future. There could be physical suffering, illness, pain and grievous loss.

How wise the Lover of our soul is to introduce myrrh to us in small, manageable amounts!

Just a little bundle. Otherwise, it would be very easy for those who have decided to follow Jesus to become overwhelmed when difficult circumstances arise.

At this early stage of her relationship, the Bride's focus is not on present or future suffering. Her attention is on this Man who is holding her in His arms. He has become very beloved. She is going to keep Him very close to her heart!

We who know the Lord Jesus understand what this young woman was feeling. How precious He is to us! His presence in our lives is an irreplaceable treasure.

14 My beloved is unto me as a cluster of camphire in the vineyards of Engedi.

Camphire, like myrrh and spikenard, is also rare, and only grows in the area of the oasis of Engedi in Israel, nourished by the pure spring water that bubbles up from under the wilderness rocks. Its flower has a beautiful aroma.

Because there are no stage directions in the margin for this ancient drama, we can't be sure if this statement was the Shepherd/King's response to her declaration of love, or if the Bride is still expounding on her Lover's wonderful attributes. I'm taking the liberty of assigning this line to the Shepherd/King as he declares that His beautiful bride is very precious to Him. Her worship and adoration is like a sweet perfume in his nostrils, and to him it is a very treasured commodity.

16 Behold, thou are fair, my beloved, yea, pleasant: also our bed is green.

As I read this statement, my mind immediately goes to one of the most-loved and oft-quoted Psalms, Psalm 23. Verse 2 states, *"He makes me to lie down in green pastures."* The love these two share is one that is full of life, growth, and expectancy. No mention is made of the barrenness of brown, or the bleakness of grey. This is not a winter season of her life but rather a time of fruitfulness and rebirth. Green represents spring, the season of new life. As she progresses in her relationship with her Lover, the Bride is beginning to understand that growth is an expectation, and that the birth of another generation is in her future.

The mention of their bed points to a level of private intimacy. These private moments are so important and valuable in any believer's life. Being in church with other believers, singing the songs of Zion, worshipping together and hearing the Word preached is a great privilege that we must never take for granted. However, those private, intimate moments with the Lover of your soul, times when it's only the two of you together, are not only precious, but very necessary. It's in the privacy of your personal time with the Lord that your knowledge of Him grows exponentially. Those nuggets from His Word that He drops into your mind at a time of need, those tears that flow in your prayer closet, those hands raised in worship in the quietness of your home - how they bless us and draw us into an intimate relationship with Him! Without this private intimacy, the relationship between the

Believer/Bride and the Shepherd/King would quickly become shallow, stagnant and stale. The intimate words and acts of love keep the relationship alive.

17. The beams of our house are cedar, and our rafters of fir.

Several years before Solomon wrote this song, his father, King David, had decided that it was time to build a permanent home for the Ark that had traveled with God's people since their time of wandering in the wilderness. 1 Chronicles 17 tells the story of how David felt grieved that he was living in a palace built of cedar while the Ark of the Covenant, with all its glory and power, was housed in a tent. He decided, with the prophet Nathan's blessing, to build a permanent dwelling place for the presence of God. But God had other ideas. He instructed Nathan to tell David that He had never asked for a house to be built for Him. His choice was to dwell in the hearts of His people. Instead, God declared in verse 10, that He was actually going to build a house for David! We could use up several pages talking about the house that God built for His people. Isn't it remarkable that Jesus was known as the carpenter's son? A builder! Jesus said He would build His church upon the solid foundation of His identity as the Christ, the Son of the living God. Paul wrote in II Corinthians 5:1 that "...we have a building of God, an house not made with hands, eternal in the heavens." The church, comprised of individuals from all across the globe, is built together as a dwelling place for the Spirit of God, and one day soon we will move to our permanent home in Heaven.

In Solomon's song the Shepherd/King prophesies of the home He will build for His beloved. A home that would not be a portable tent, like the one the Children of Israel followed in the wilderness, but a permanent home that would be secure and protected from the elements, with beams of cedar and rafters of fir. This peasant girl from the vineyard may have grown up poor, on the wrong side of the tracks, but her new address would be a beautiful custom-built palace.

2:1 I am the rose of Sharon, and the lily of the valleys.

Continuing their loving conversation, the Bride shyly says that she finds it hard to believe she will be the recipient of such amazing blessings. In her own mind, she is not anything special. She is aware that members of her family are just simple, common labourers, working for a wealthy landowner. She blushes as she says, 'Just as the plains of Sharon are covered with blossoms in the spring, and just as the valleys are filled with lilies, I am only one of thousands that are all the same.' How can she accept that she is seen by her Lover as someone unique?

I identify with that sentiment, and I'm quite sure that most readers would feel the same. There are believers in Jesus all over the world. Some of them are mightily used in the Kingdom of God and others are at this moment suffering terrible persecution. There are Jesus-followers who need miraculous, physical healing, and many who are walking through very difficult times of persecution. There are Believers with great talents and abilities. Who am I among so many? Why would I think it's permissible for me to take up Jesus' time with my every-day issues and problems when there are so many others with needs that are much more pressing than mine, and so many who are much more useful to His Kingdom than I could ever be? I am one lily in a valley filled with lilies.

But then His loving voice reminds me of my value to Him:

2 As the lily among thorns, so is my love among the daughters.

The Shepherd/King's response comes back loud and clear: you are not just one of many, anonymous and unnoticed. You are not just another face in the crowd. From the Shepherd/King's perspective, this one He loves is a magnificent lily in a field filled with thorns, standing out from the crowd, unique and beautiful. In Japan, in Bolivia, in Nigeria, in Papau New Guinea, in Latvia, in Thailand, in Argentina, in Mexico, in Saudi Arabia, in Australia, in fact, all over the world, there are distinctive, much-loved "lilies" growing under the watchful care of their Lover, the Lord Jesus. He knows and loves each one individually.

Each one of us holds a very special place in the heart of our Saviour, Jesus. Phrases such as "the apple of his eye" come to mind. Jesus told his disciples that a sparrow doesn't fall to the ground without the notice of His Father. How much more valuable am I than a sparrow? None of us should ever perceive ourselves as unnoticed and without any value. He sees each one of us individually as His Beloved.

End of Act I, Scene I

Act I, Scene IV
Provision
Song of Solomon 2:4

4 He brought me to the banqueting house, and his banner over me was love.

As the curtain rises again, we can see that the stage hands have been very busy. The stage is now filled with a huge table, loaded down with every delectable treat imaginable. Delicious aromas and tantalising scents waft throughout the audience. Revelation has dawned in the maiden's mind: In this new life I'm living, I am not going to have to beg continually for just enough food to ward off starvation, but everything I could ever need or desire has been provided for me. There are no limits and no restrictions! The supply from God's throne is not doled out by spoonfuls. There has been an abundant *banquet* of blessings and provision prepared for us.

There is, however, much more spread out on this table than blessings and immediate provision of our daily needs. Yes, Jesus instructed his disciples to pray for their *daily* bread, since having our daily needs met is an effect of being part of His family, but He also guided them to pray for His Kingdom to come and His will to be done on earth!

Sadly, so many believers only ever satisfy their basic hunger for a shallow experience with Jesus, without ever understanding that there is so much more available to them. They seem to survive (barely) on a "good feeling" in a Sunday morning service without understanding that they are not being spiritually nourished with that once-a-week encounter with the Lord.

On that banquet table is the invitation for a deep and intimate walk with our Saviour. The possibilities are endless - hearing His voice directing your decisions, praying in the Spirit, being led by that same Spirit as you navigate through the ups and downs of life, feeling His presence in your home, having His Word come alive to you as you privately study and meditate, being used to minister to someone else's need, having His words in your conversations because those words have become a part of you as you live in Him.

Don't be satisfied with cookies and cupcakes when you have so much more available to you! O taste and see that the Lord is good!

A banner is a standard that bears the colours by which a military unit is identified and behind which troops rally. The "standard-bearer" carries the banner proudly in a celebratory parade. Marching bands are often preceded by their leader carrying the banner that identifies their unit. The musicians march in formation behind the banner.

At this banquet we are all invited to, the identifying banner has one word written on it: LOVE. We belong to a body of believers, marching in one accord behind Jesus. He declared, "By this shall all men know that ye are my disciples, if ye have *love* one to another." (John 13:35).

The banner over the church is LOVE. His love for us, our love for Him, and as an extension, our love for each other and for the world.

And so, we come to the end of this first "new convert" phase of the Believer's experience. As Winston Churchill declared in 1942, during the Second World War, "This is not the end, this is not even the beginning of the end, this is just perhaps the end of the beginning." The Believer/Bride has a long road in front of her. Many experiences are to come that will teach her to depend on the Shepherd, experiences that will teach her not to take for granted the blessings she has been given. Experiences where she will learn the expectation for her achievement is high. Experiences that will bring clear understanding that her priority should not only be blessing and provision, but that the most important thing in her life is hearing the voice of her Lover and following wherever He leads.

End of Act I, Scene IV

Rise up, My Love, And Come Away

ACT II

Act II, Scene I
Invitation to a Journey
Song of Solomon 2:8-14

In this second act, a shift has taken place in the relationship between the Shepherd/King and His Bride. Until now the emphasis has been on provision for her needs and a loving introduction to the concept of worship. The Bride has shown that she is very content to remain in this comfortable position of embracing her Beloved, with all her needs being met. But now we will be introduced to a new aspect of the Shepherd/King. *He is a man of action.* His character is not satisfied to simply rest and relax continually. His knowledge of the world beyond the vineyard where He discovered the sweet peasant maiden is vast, and there is so much He wants to show her and share with her.

It could be tempting for a new convert to stay at that infant stage where it's all about provision and pleasure, but that's not what our Lord Jesus intends for us. He can't wait to lead us into new places we've never been before because the boundaries of our experience had never been stretched. He wants to challenge us to explore His Word, to step out in faith, to grow in knowledge, to become strong and mature believers.

Jesus, our Shepherd/King, leads us step by step and experience by experience into these new territories. Sadly, there are many Christian believers who never get past Act I. They remain immature and irresponsible, easily offended, easily distracted, easily miss church services for any reason, easily say no when asked to participate at a deeper level. Instead, they live their entire spiritual lives only concerned with having their needs met. Satisfied to have a blessing on Sunday morning. I don't want to be that person! I want to experience everything that my Beloved Saviour and Lord has for me.

> *8 The voice of my beloved! behold, he comes leaping upon the mountains, skipping upon the hills.*

There is a light, festive, joyful feeling at the beginning of the first scene of this second act. The Bride says, I hear my Beloved's voice! He is on His way to me, and no hindrance is going to slow Him down. He simply leaps and skips over the mountains and across the valleys. This is not a time for weeping or mourning. This is a time to celebrate our love!

What an awesome, amazing experience it is to hear the voice of your Beloved. What an awesome, amazing privilege it is to hear that sweet voice speaking in your ear and your heart!

I have heard that voice giving me specific direction for my life when I was confused. I have heard the voice of my Beloved challenging me to go beyond any sacrifice I had made up to that point in my life. I have heard His voice when I've made mistakes, as he gently chided me while leading me back to the right path. His voice has brought comfort to my hurting heart. His voice has encouraged me when I felt like a failure.

Sometimes the voice speaks clearly to me as I read the Word. Other times the voice sounds very much like my pastor, or my husband, or a dear, concerned friend. Sometimes the voice is simply an urging or a prompting in my heart as I seek Jesus in prayer. How thankful I am for His voice, the voice of my Beloved!

Perhaps the Bride's immature expectation has been that life would continue as it had been in the first act, when she was a brand new Believer. But she is in for a surprise! The Bridegroom has other ideas and plans.

9 My beloved is like a roe or a young hart: behold, he stands behind our wall, he looks forth at the windows, shewing himself through the lattice.

We in the audience watch closely as this subtle shift takes place in the relationship between the Shepherd and His Bride. He is ready to show her things she has never seen before, while, unaware of His plans, she stands and watches His approach, admiring His strength and vitality and revelling in the anticipation of His love. However, instead of entering their home as she expected He would, He remains outside, almost out of view.

Lovingly He peeks through the windowpane, seeking her attention, enticing her to come out of the safety of the present location she is accustomed to, to go exploring with Him. Is she ready for this adventure? Is she ready to leave the comfort of His provision and blessing to see and experience new vistas?

> *10. My beloved spake, and said unto me, Rise up, my love, my fair one, and come away.*

The Beloved Shepherd/King makes it clear that it's time for a change in this relationship. Yes, He declares, I am your beloved, and I always will be. You are my love, and that will always remain the same. But there is much more that I want to show you! I want to take you to new places that you've never been to before. I want to broaden your horizons. Come walk with me, my Bride. Rise up from your comfortable place and come away with me! Take up the challenge of moving beyond blessing and provision, and follow me into new and thrilling territory!

This phrase contains four very important principles for us to follow and understand as we go deeper into our relationship with Jesus:

Rise up!

It seems so obvious, but we're not going to be able to move forward or go deeper as long as we stay in the same comfortable position we've been in for a while. "Rise up," says the Shepherd/King. Get ready for action. Don't get ahead of me but be ready to move at a moment's notice.

My Love!

Oh, if only all of us as believers could grasp this concept. We are His love! We are not His project. We are not His assignment. We are *His love*. So often we believers go through our daily lives feeling fear that we are about to be punished or judged for some misdemeanour. We sing songs about joy but we don't *live* in joy very often because we have never completely grasped the breadth, the length, the depth and height of God's love for us.

My Fair One!

God's perspective of us is quite different from our own view of ourself! We see all our faults, all our carnal thoughts and actions. We know ourselves quite well. We are continually reminded by the enemy of our soul that we are sinners. "You'll never amount to anything!" he repeatedly reminds us. But when God looks at us, He sees us covered by the perfect blood of Jesus. To Him, we are beautiful. We are His "fair one." Tell yourself over and over again, "I am His fair one." He sees a beauty in me that no one else ever saw.

Come Away!

And there's the catch. How hungry are you to know your Shepherd/King? Are you hungry enough to leave behind the comfort of the known? Are you hungry enough to step away from the crowd? Are you hungry enough to spend hours, just Him and you, digging into His Word? Come away, He says. Let me take you places that others won't or can't go. Oh, there's so much He has for you! He has treasures, precious, private moments, personal messages...but you have to take the risk, you have to "come away."

11 - 13 For lo, the winter is past, the rain is over and gone; the flowers appear on the earth, the time of the singing of birds is come, and the voice of the turtle is heard in our land; the fig tree puts forth her green figs, and the vines with the tender grape give a good smell. Arise, my love, my fair one, and come away.

The backdrop on the stage for this scene is beautiful. The sky is blue and cloudless. The birds are singing, the tree branches that had been bare and stark are now green with the promise of new growth. Everywhere you look there are flowers. It's a new season! It's SPRINGTIME! It's the time for growth. It's the time for new life. It's so exciting, especially after long, bleak months of drizzling rain and bone-aching cold. For the Bride who has grown accustomed to blessing and provision, it's time for new revelation. The Bridegroom is introducing His Beloved to the concept, which will be recurring, of growth. Write this down: In this relationship with the Shepherd/King there will *always* be the expectation of fruitfulness.

The Bride feels the excitement of the moment and soon she is out the door, hand outstretched to the Beloved's, ready for this new experience. Let's go! I'm ready for this spring-time adventure!

This new level in their relationship with Jesus is such a blessed time for a new believer and convert! No longer satisfied with only an emotional experience, they happily embrace this new season of growth, showing up for Bible Study and prayer meeting, digging into the Word, putting down roots down in the church. Those of us who have already passed this stage in our own personal experience with Jesus watch their progress with joy. There aren't too many things more exciting than having new Jesus-followers filling the front pews in a church on Bible Study night!

The green figs and tender grapes mentioned in this passage indicate that the relationship, although deepening, is still at a relatively immature level. There are definite signs of growth, though, and that's what is important for now.

There is never an expectation for ripened fruit in the springtime. All gardeners and farmers know there is a process of time that has to take place between the appearance of tiny buds on the vines and the juicy figs and ripe grapes that are ready to be harvested several weeks later. How often the mistake is made of expecting a new convert to display signs of maturity. How often a new believer is pressured to fulfill unrealistic expectations. Thankfully the Lord of the Harvest knows that it will take time and He is patient with the process. Why is it that we so often fall into the trap of judging the result when there has not been enough time for the fruit to grow?

14. O my dove, that art in the clefts of the rock, in the secret places of the stairs, let me see thy countenance, let me hear thy voice; for sweet is thy voice, and thy countenance is comely.

You already know that we don't live our every day lives on the level of leaping and skipping and banqueting. Real life kicks in, and there are times when it feels overwhelmingly difficult to even put one foot in front of the other, never mind trying to leap and skip over mountains!

As they proceed together on this spring-time adventure, the Bride follows her Lover's lead. His intention is to guide her into a new experience of trust. In an unexpected twist that she finds quite upsetting, He squeezes into a narrow cave where there are stairs that have been carved into the rock. The purpose of the stairs is to provide access to the mountaintop to anyone who would venture into this cavern.

Being in the dark cave for the first time is daunting. It's definitely not what the Bride expected when her Bridegroom stood outside her window and beckoned her to come away with Him. Sunlight doesn't penetrate the cave and she has to follow blindly, trusting that He is leading her to a good outcome.

Her response is childlike. I don't like it when I can't see your face and hear your voice. You know that I love listening to your voice and watching your face as we share loving secrets. This detour into a dark cave isn't comfortable for me. Why are You bringing me here?

In our walk with God, there will be times when He leads us into unfamiliar territory. We may find ourselves in a difficult place, perhaps the loss of a job or a broken relationship. Suddenly we have to blindly trust Him because the path is not clear. It's easy to begin to doubt and question. Am I out of the will of God? Have I sinned? Has the Lord abandoned me to walk alone?

Sadly, many new believers reach this stage in their relationship with Jesus and turn back, because this new level of experience is too challenging for them. They loved having their needs met, they loved learning to rest in His presence. They loved standing at the banqueting table where so many delicious, nourishing foods have been prepared for them. But this frightening feeling is not what they bargained for. They petulantly ask, "Why isn't He speaking to me? Why can't I see Him clearly?" That wonderful banqueting table of blessing has been whisked off the stage and has been replaced by a craggy mountain that is very demanding. As a result, they convince themselves that turning back is the best option.

If you find yourself in a dark, confined cave, unsure of where you should go next, don't give up! Don't start looking for the closest exit. Instead, if you are in a place where you're not sure which direction you should take, hold on tightly to the Beloved's hand, and allow Him to lead you forward, even if you are only taking small steps! Don't ever turn around and retreat!

There are tremendous benefits to those who follow their Lover into the clefts of the rock.

Moses experienced God's glory as it passed by Him, hidden in the cleft. God promised Him, "And it shall come to pass, while my glory passeth by, that I will put thee in a cleft of the rock, and will cover thee with my hand while I pass by" (Exodus 33:22).

Through the chief Musician Asaph, God expressed the reward that is available to us if we follow Him, "Oh that my people had hearkened unto me, and Israel had walked in my ways! I should soon have subdued their enemies, and turned my hand against their adversaries. The haters of the Lord should have submitted themselves unto him: but their time should have endured forever. He should have fed them also with the finest of the wheat: *and with honey out of the rock should I have satisfied thee*" (Psalm 81:13-16).

Paul said it so perfectly in II Corinthians 4:17-18, "Our light affliction, *which is but for a moment*, works for us a far more exceeding and eternal weight of glory." Those dark moments in the cave didn't happen because you made a mistake. They happened because the Lover of your soul wanted to lead you to a higher level of spiritual understanding. He wanted you to experience His trustworthiness. If you make up your mind to hearken to His voice, and walk in His ways, even if it involves dark caves and uneven stone stairs, you will ultimately enjoy not only His special brand of honey and gourmet bread, but you will experience your Champion fighting for you, and you will have the promise of eternal life.

The Shepherd had no intention of abandoning His Bride to hopelessly wander through the dark crevices of the rock. He simply wanted her to learn that she could trust Him in every situation.

Before the curtain closes on this scene, let's talk briefly about the secret places of the stairs.

I have an interesting note in the margin of this page in my Bible that I wrote during my private Bible study: There is no elevator to success; you have to take the stairs.

Stairs go in both directions, up and down. If you have a desire to climb to the mountaintops of experience and understanding in the Kingdom of God, there will be times when the only way to move forward is by the stairs. One step at a time. Not running or leaping, but cautiously putting one foot on the next level, and then the next, and the next.

It's relatively simple to *say*, "I want to be more spiritual," "I want to be a prayer warrior," "I want to be effective in the Kingdom of God." However, in order for this to happen in a believer's life, there are secret places of stairs that will be traversed. There will be times of deep suffering. Times of humiliation. Times of loneliness, when His voice is very faint. Times when it feels like there is nowhere to go but down. Times when you find yourself flat on your face, broken by the trying circumstances you are going through. Most of those struggles are in secret. The pain is private. When we're out in public we wear a plastic, professional smile so that no one will know how much we are struggling in the secret places of the stairs.

Strangely, though, because God's Kingdom operates differently from worldly kingdoms, it is after those deep trials the discovery is made that, rather than going lower and lower, as was thought, the Believer was actually climbing higher and higher. Perhaps there are a few bruises on her shins because she stumbled on a step. Perhaps she is cradling her arm that suffered a sprain as she slipped and fell. But what a pleasant surprise awaits her! The Shepherd/King was there all the time and as they emerge together from the secret places into the spring sunshine, the view is very different than before because the stairs inside the cleft of the rock have taken them to a much higher level.

It is these difficult, dark times that teach the Believer to hold onto the Shepherd's hand with trust that He will lead her out of the darkness. The Bride is learning that she can trust her Lover to lead her through the dark, difficult places. He is trustworthy! He promised that He would never leave or forsake her. Their relationship is growing deeper as a result of these experiences.

As we come to the close of this first scene in Act II, we can see that the Believer/Bride is making steady progress in her walk with God. She has passed the stage of only wanting blessing and provision; she has learned how to worship through times of suffering, and now she has entered a new level of trust and confidence in her Lover. It will be interesting to see what happens next!

End of Act II, Scene I

Act II
Interlude
Song of Solomon 2:15

Before the curtains open for the next scene, the director steps onto the stage to make an announcement.

I'm reminded of dramas that we attended during the years our children were in school. Often times during a scene change the director would slip onto the stage to announce that there was a car in the parking lot with its lights on, or to kindly suggest that everyone in the audience please turn off their phone.

In this poetic drama that King Solomon wrote, between scenes of the splendour of spring and the challenge of mountain climbing, the director stands up to make an announcement and issue a warning:

> 15 Take us the foxes, the little foxes, that spoil the vines: for our vines have tender grapes.

In this environment of growth and progress towards spiritual maturity, you will always need to be on the alert for *little* foxes that spoil the vine.

The thing is, full-grown foxes and other large-bodied predators are very obvious. Foxes aren't particularly large animals, but when full-grown, they don't slip by unnoticed. But *little* foxes, well, that's another matter altogether. Because of their size, you wonder if your eyes were deceiving you…did you really see something scoot under that shrub? Or was it a shadow? Sadly, those *little* foxes can wiggle under the vines without detection, and can nibble away at the tiny sprouts, destroying the new growth before it ever gets a chance to ripen.

Those big foxes, like lying, cheating, stealing, violent anger, adultery or abuse, are all easily detected and can be dealt with through prayer and repentance, and sometimes severe punishment. Little foxes, though, like gossip, complaining, criticism, taking or giving offence and unforgiveness are much less obvious, and they have the ability to manoeuvre their way into our hearts and spirits undetected until, before we realize what's happened, they have gnawed away at our faith and our confidence in God. Without sincere repentance, eventually the budding, tender fruit disappears and all that remains are bare stems and branches.

Healthy relationships are not automatic. Whether it's a relationship between a husband and a wife, parents and their children, colleagues at a place of employment, or a believer and Jesus, a healthy, growing relationship will take effort. None of us can afford to allow little foxes to wriggle under the fence and wreak havoc. Guard your heart at all times. Keep the fences mended. Watch out for those trouble-making little foxes!

End of Interlude

Act II, Scene II
The Journey Continues
Song of Solomon 3:1-4

1 By night on my bed I sought him whom my soul loveth: I sought him, but I found Him not.

The Bride has continued to make steady progress in her spiritual journey. In the early moments of passionate infatuation in the first scene of Act I, she found nourishment and rest, then moved on to an intimate embrace before heading out with her Beloved on an adventure in the spring sunshine.

As the curtain rises again, the first thing we notice is that the sun has disappeared and we now find ourselves in the darkness of night.

Wouldn't it be wonderful if the sun could just keep shining and we never had to face those dark moments of life? How amazing would it be if we could continually skip and leap over mountains in the fresh air of springtime?

Sadly, life doesn't work that way. In the natural, there has been a cycle of darkness and light since the earth was first created. It happens every single day. There was one occasion a few thousand years ago when nightfall was postponed while the armies of the Lord fought a very important battle, but even on that very unique day, the sun eventually set in the west and darkness fell.

In the world of horticulture, during the day plants absorb energy from the sun and use it to convert water, carbon dioxide and minerals into oxygen and other organic compounds. In other words, the plants are working all day producing the oxygen that humans need to survive. This process is called photosynthesis. But once darkness falls, photosynthesis stops. For the next several hours all plants, whether it's a little petunia in someone's window-box, or a vast field of soybeans in Iowa, use the energy from the sun that they've stored, to grow. And growth is good! Growth is the desired outcome. Oxygen, a requirement for human and animal life, is the product of photosynthesis. When He created the world, God established an amazing balance between humans and nature. But I guarantee that most farmers and gardeners are not thinking about the production of oxygen when they plant their rows of beans or fields of corn. Every gardener and every farmer knows that the priority for that vegetable patch or sown field is *growth*. Seeds hidden in the earth do not feed the masses.

In our walk with the Lord, it is inevitable that times of blessing and refreshing will be followed by dark periods. There will be moments when we either intentionally rest and regroup or moments when unavoidable circumstances force us to stop our activity. It is during those night seasons that real growth commences and our roots deepen into the soil.

The new Bride is unsettled by being alone in the darkness of night. Accustomed as she is to the companionship of her Beloved, she reaches out to be reassured by His familiar touch. To her surprise, He is beyond her outstretched hand. In fact, He doesn't seem to be nearby at all. Her reaction is immediate:

2 I will rise now; and go about the city in the streets, and in the broad ways I will seek him whom my soul loveth: I sought him, but I found him not.

For new and inexperienced believers, this phenomenon causes panic the first time it occurs. Oh no, I've been abandoned! It's dark! I need my Beloved here beside me to make sure everything is all right again. Not realising that the darkness is only temporary, that the sun will be rising again in a few hours and that the Bridegroom is really not far away, they rush around, going here and there, looking in all the wrong places, busy streets and broad ways, to get that passionate feeling back again. However, in her defence and on a positive note, in this verse the Bride at least takes action to ensure the Bridegroom is located.

The broad way seems to be the default road that most people travel. But a deep relationship with Jesus won't be developed on the busy highway where there are constant distractions. If your desire is to find and know Him, you should look for Him off the beaten track, where you will probably be traveling alone. The likelihood of finding Him is much higher on the less-traveled ways than on the busy thoroughfares of the world.

The Bride wastes valuable time running here and there, looking for that familiar feeling.

> *3 - 4a The watchmen that go about the city found me: to whom I said, Saw ye him whom my soul loveth? It was but a little that I passed from them, but I found him whom my soul loveth.*

Fortunately for the Bride, she found some kind watchmen who steered her in the right direction, away from the broad ways, and in just a little while she was reunited with the Lover of her soul. She didn't have to go far to find Him! He'd been close by all the time.

The night experience had been what we used to call in high school, a "pop-quiz", a brief test to see how she would react to a challenging situation. She was blessed on this occasion that there were good watchmen from whom she could ask directions. What tremendous value there is in a pastor whose guidance with those new and unstable believers is gentle and reassuring rather than filled with judgment and condemnation!

4b I held him, and would not let him go, until I had brought him into my mother's house, and into the chamber of her that conceived me.

There is no comparison to the sensation of once again feeling the powerful presence of Jesus moving in your spirit after a time of trial and testing!

As a result of this experience she has just gone through, the Bride has a new determination that she is going to "hang on for dear life" to the Shepherd/King. That's a good outcome!

The Believer knows exactly where she needs to go next. I'm taking you *home,* she says. We're going back to my mother's house, to the place where my spiritual birth occurred. We're going back to the moment when the seed of the Word dropped into my heart and where, upon colliding with the measure of faith that God had placed there, conception occurred. We're going back to the family, to the place where, as a newborn, I was nurtured and cared for.

In our spiritual journey, there is potential to travel to deep depths and high heights in the Spirit. The possibilities are endless, because, as Ephesians 3:20 says, He is able to do exceeding abundantly above all that we can ask or even think! Don't forget though, that it's *according to the power that works in us.* We set the pace and determine the limits of how far we want to go in this amazing experience. However, it's important that we always stay connected to our roots. We need the family of God surrounding us. Don't ever make the mistake of deciding you can make it on your own, because you can't and you won't. Plain and simple.

In this moment of clarity, the Believer/Bride teeters on the edge of a giant leap into the next act. As the curtain drops on the second act, the Bride comes to the understanding that the chamber where *she* was conceived is *still* the chamber of reproduction. The process didn't stop with her; it is an on-going one.

We will enter the chamber together, my Lover and I, and we will reproduce the next generation of believers. I'm not an immature child anymore, requiring someone else to feed me and take care of me. I actually have a responsibility to birth more babies into this family!

End of Act II, Scene II

Rise up, My Love, And Come Away

ACT III

Act III, Scene I
Revelation
Song of Solomon 3:6-11

6 Who is this that cometh out of the wilderness like pillars of smoke, perfumed with myrrh and frankincense, with all powders of the merchant?

Oh, I just LOVE this part of the story! The stage curtains open on an absolutely spectacular scene. The Bride stands with shock and amazement on her face as she gazes on the drama unfolding in front of her. She turns and asks the audience, "Who is this coming out of the wilderness?" She recognises Him as her Lover and as the gentle Shepherd she fell in love with, but what she is seeing in this moment is revelatory!

The pillars of smoke, the perfume of myrrh and frankincense, and the powders of the merchant hold great significance in the Bride's understanding of Who this person really is.

Our precious Saviour, Jesus Christ, spent forty days in the wilderness at the beginning of His earthly ministry. He was tempted by His enemy, Satan, and overcame him. He was ministered to by angels as he wrestled with demonic forces. After the forty days were completed, *he came out of that wilderness* in the power of the Spirit. A few days later He showed up in the synagogue in Nazareth, and made the powerful declaration, "The Spirit of the Lord is upon me, *because he has anointed me to preach the gospel to the poor; he has sent me to heal the broken-hearted, to preach deliverance to the captives, and recovering of sight to the blind, to set at liberty them that are bruised, to preach the acceptable year of the Lord"* (Luke 4:18-19).

In this first scene of the third act, the Believer/Bride sees her Beloved on the stage, surrounded by pillars of smoke. Not just a little puff of smoke, mind you, but smoke that fills her vision. Revelation 15:8 explains to us what is happening here: "And the temple was filled with smoke from the glory of God, and from his power." The Bride is seeing, for the first time, the Glory of God that rests upon her Beloved. John wrote about it like this in his gospel: "And the Word was made flesh, and dwelt among us, (and we beheld his glory, the glory as of the only begotten of the Father), full of grace and truth" (John 1:14). The Bride is awe-struck as she beholds her Lover with the Glory of God upon Him. He is no longer only a kind and gentle Shepherd but Someone upon whom God's glory rests, and through whom God's omnipotence flows. There is an air of majesty about Him.

He has been perfumed (anointed) with myrrh and frankincense, foreshadows first of the suffering He will endure at the time when His earthly ministry is completed, and ultimately of the worship He will receive when He is crowned as King of Kings and Lord of Lords.

At the time when Solomon wrote his prophetic song, anointing was reserved for kings and priests. Aaron was anointed as the High Priest by Moses. The prophet Samuel anointed Saul to be the first king over Israel, and then, a few years later, in a story that's very familiar to most of us, Samuel anointed the young shepherd boy, David, the son of Jesse, to be King.

As her Lover emerges from the wilderness, the heady perfume of the anointing oil upon Him announces emphatically to the Bride that He is not only a lowly shepherd, but a powerful King surrounded by the glory of God. What an incredible revelation! She is reaching a place of comprehending not just His wonderful love, but also His power and authority.

In His hands are all the powders of the merchant. Merchants sell products that customers require. What things do every one of us believers need? We need salvation, healing, peace, restoration, joy, comfort, strength, wisdom and counsel. All of the items on that list are available to us through Him. In fact, anything you might ever need can be found in His hands.

The Jews believed that their Messiah would be revealed coming out of the wilderness as a crowned King and a Mighty Deliverer who would set them free from all oppressors. When Jesus arrived on the scene, several boxes of Messianic prophecies were ticked, such as his birthplace in Bethlehem to a virgin maiden. But as time passed, He disappointed them by His meekness. He certainly didn't conduct Himself like a mighty warrior! His disciples who walked with Him daily continually pestered Jesus about the timing of Him setting up His

Kingdom, even in the last moments just before His ascension into the heavens from the Mount of Olives. Ultimately Jesus was rejected by the Jews as their Messiah because they could not accept His insistence on suffering and finally giving His life as the sacrificial Lamb.

Oh, the joy for us who have believed in Him, to understand that Jesus will one day be revealed as King over all the earth. "That at the name of Jesus *every knee should bow...* and that every tongue should confess that Jesus Christ is Lord, to the glory of God the Father" (Philippians 2:10-11).

Another wilderness followed that sojourn into the desert place at the beginning of His ministry. To fulfil God's plan that had been put In place from the foundation of the world, Jesus entered the wilderness of death. He was stripped, beaten, mocked, abandoned by His disciples and finally nailed to the wooden cross. He cried aloud to His Father, Why have You forsaken me?

He suffered and gave His life in exchange for ours. He went into the wilderness of death.

His battered body was gently wrapped by His heartbroken followers and laid in a borrowed tomb. He went into Hell, where he wrestled the keys of death and hell away from Satan.

He didn't stay in that wilderness, though. The stone that had been placed at the entrance to the tomb, just in case His disciples tried to sneak his body away and pretend He had resurrected, was rolled away by an angel, and Jesus stepped out into the bright morning sunshine, the scent of the garden flowers filling the air. He was triumphant over death. He now rules as King over a Kingdom that shall have no end. He is alive forevermore. And one of these days every eye will behold Him and acknowledge His identity.

The question may be asked, "Who is this coming out of the wilderness?" The answer will be, it is Jesus Christ, the King of Glory. He is no longer just a humble Shepherd. He is the Lord of lords, the King of kings, the Alpha, the Omega, the Beginning and the End.

It is absolutely essential for every Believer who wants to grow to higher levels of maturity to have a moment in their life where the light of revelation shines into their heart, their mind and their spirit. A moment when they grasp the truth of the identity of Jesus Christ: Yes, He is a gentle Shepherd. Yes, His presence is sweet and wonderful. Yes, He is patiently leading me to deeper depths and higher heights of spiritual understanding. Yes, these things are true. But He's much more than that. He is that child that Isaiah prophesied would be born, whose name is Wonderful, Counselor, The Mighty God, the Everlasting Father, the Prince of Peace. Jesus Christ is God, manifested in flesh. He is the Word of God, that first voice that was ever heard in eternity, made flesh and dwelling among us, humanity and divinity walking on calloused feet through the hills and byways of Judea. God, Who is the omnipresent, omnipotent, omniscient One. The majestic One. The God who said through the prophet Isaiah, "I am the Lord, and there is none else, there is no God beside me: I girded thee, though thou hast not known me: That they may know from the rising of the sun, and from the west, that there is none beside me. I am the Lord, and there is none else" (Isaiah 45:5-6). Jesus said,

"If you believe not that I am He, you shall die in your sins" (John 8:24). He's more than a story...He's the King of Glory!

The day is coming soon when not only we who are His Beloved Bride understand who He is, but the entire world will know. He will be revealed as the Messiah of the Jews, the Allah of the Muslims, the "Unknown God" of the Greeks, and the true God that every man-made religion has tried to obliterate with their idols. What a glorious day that will be!

7 Behold his bed, which is Solomon's; three-score valiant men are about it, of the valiant of Israel.

The Bride now has understanding and revelation of the identity of this man with whom she has fallen in love. As if she is giving us a guided tour of His palace, she points out to us the kingly furniture, specifically Solomon's bed, as proof of His identity.

We are introduced at this point to sixty valiant men of Israel who accompany the King everywhere He goes. I believe this scene has a dual interpretation. First of all, we are encountering the host of angels who are heavenly warriors in the Kingdom of God, fighting on our behalf against attacks of the enemy Satan. However, the application goes further than that. In this Kingdom that we have become a part of, we are *all* expected to learn the art of spiritual warfare. Jesus declared in Matthew 11:12 that His Kingdom allowed violence, and that the violent would take it by force. As the church battles against the forces of evil, the gates of Hell will not be able to withstand the assault, and prisoners who have been captured and incarcerated by the wiles of the devil will be set free.

8 They all hold swords, being expert in war: every man has his sword upon his thigh because of fear in the night.

Warriors! I love the description that is given of these valiant men, whether heavenly angels or earthly believers: they are *experts* in war. They are not timid or inexperienced in battle. They are not intimidated by anything the devil tries to do. They are not ignorant of his devices. These valiant men have fought many battles and they are experts, with the sword of the Spirit readily available to engage with the enemy. They are intimately knowledgeable of the power of the Word. They are ready at a moment's notice to protect the body of Christ, to defend God's Kingdom, and to go on the offensive against the wiles of the enemy.

There's an interesting interaction between Jesus and His disciples recorded in Luke 22:35-36. It takes place at the conclusion of the last supper, as they proceed from that upper room to the Garden of Gethsemane, where Jesus will soon be arrested.

"And He said unto them, 'When I sent you without purse, and scrip, and shoes, lacked ye anything?' And they said, 'Nothing'. Then said he unto them, 'But now, he that hath a purse, let him take it, and likewise his scrip: and *he that hath no sword, let him sell his garment, and buy one.*"

Earlier, Luke had written how Jesus sent His disciples out on an evangelistic tour. At that time, those twelve men were young, inexperienced and very immature. Jesus' instructions meant they were going to learn to depend completely on God's provision for them. It was a very specific learning experience.

But by the 22nd chapter, much has changed. The disciples had been given great revelation. It was time for them to assume the reigns of leadership of the church that would be born a few days hence, and so Jesus' instructions also changed. He told them in no uncertain terms that *they were going to need a sword*, even if it meant they had to sell the very shirt off their back in order to have enough funds to buy one. Still not fully comprehending, someone ran back into the room they had just left, rummaged around in a cupboard and amazingly, found two swords which were brought to Jesus in a great flurry of excitement.

But Jesus hadn't meant they needed a sword they could use to chop off an enemy's ear, as happened a couple of hours later. Jesus was telling them that the bar was much higher now, His expectation of them was much more. They had to become men of war. Their sphere of influence would be *the world,* not just a few nearby villages. His intention was for them to finally understand that they would be warriors, experts in the art of spiritual warfare. More than anything else, they needed to have their sword ready at all times.

Whether they had a fancy jacket to wear or not wouldn't really matter, but in the many situations and circumstances those men who were so dear to Him would find themselves in the coming years, a sharpened sword, ready at a moment's notice, was absolutely essential.

Perhaps the young, and still relatively immature Believer/Bride didn't fully comprehend the significance of those men of war having a sword that was readily available. However, we who are filled with the Spirit and who are consistently growing and maturing in our walk with the Shepherd/King can and must grasp this truth, that there are weapons available to us in our battle against the enemy of our soul. Get yourself a sword!

End of Act III Scene I

Act III, Scene II
Continued Revelation
Song of Solomon 3:9-11

9 King Solomon made himself a chariot of the wood of Lebanon.

The audience's attention is captured again as an incredibly beautiful chariot is rolled onto the stage.

A chariot, at its most basic definition, is a vehicle, a means of transport. However, it is not a vehicle to be used on a daily basis for ordinary excursions to the shopping mall or to pick up the children from school. Rather, a chariot is a unique vehicle that would most probably be used to carry a king for his coronation, or a conquering general as he returns victorious from battle.

King Solomon's vehicle of choice in his Song of Songs was a chariot, because he was prophetically portraying Jesus Christ, the King of Kings and the Lord of Lords, the mighty Ruler of the universe, the Champion who would conquer sin, hell and the grave, as He traveled from the portals of Heaven to the very imperfect earth where he was born to a virgin in the little town of Bethlehem.

Students of Biblical typology understand that wood depicts humanity and gold depicts divinity. In the Tabernacle that Moses built very specifically according to God's directions, the furniture pieces in the Holy Place were constructed of wood and then overlaid with gold. This was a foreshadowing of the humanity and divinity of Jesus Christ.

Philippians 2:5-8 declares, "Let this mind be in you, which was also in Christ Jesus: Who, being in the form of God, thought it not robbery to be equal with God: but *made himself* of no reputation, and took upon him the form of a servant, and *was made in the likeness of men*: and being found in fashion as a man, he humbled himself, and became obedient unto death, even the death of the cross".

Solomon wrote, "King Solomon *made himself* a chariot of the wood of Lebanon". God very intentionally robed Himself in flesh and traveled from heaven to earth in a chariot of humanity. Wood overlaid with gold. Oh, how He loves you and me! Oh, the lengths He was willing to go to reach us!

This little verse is an absolutely exquisite jewel revealing the doctrine of Jesus Christ, God manifested in flesh. The eternal, omniscient, omnipotent God of the universe robed Himself in human flesh and traveled from Heaven to earth so He could give His life in exchange for ours at Calvary.

10 He made the pillars thereof of silver, the bottom thereof of gold, the covering of it of purple, the midst thereof being paved with love, for the daughters of Jerusalem.

The framework of the chariot is silver. Silver, as a means of buying and selling, typifies redemption in the scripture. We were "redeemed", or bought back from satan who treacherously stole the human race in the garden of Eden, by the precious blood of Jesus. As His flesh was ripped by the nails and the spear, and as His perfect blood poured out on the rocks of Mount Golgotha, Jesus purchased our redemption. The Gospel of Jesus Christ, which is the framework of our faith, is the story of redemption. Pillars of silver!

The bottom, or foundation of the chariot, is gold. In Matthew 16:16, Peter boldly declared, "Thou art the Christ, the Son of the Living God." Jesus replied in verse 18, "Upon this rock (foundation) I will build my church." His church will be built on the foundation of the revelation of the divinity of Jesus Christ.

The covering of this heavenly chariot is purple. Purple is the colour of royalty. As John declared in his revelation of Jesus Christ that was given to him on the island of Patmos, "On his thigh a name written, KING OF KINGS, AND LORD OF LORDS" (Revelation 19:16). Royalty! In Isaiah 9:6, the prophet wrote, "For unto us a child is born, unto us a son is given: and the government shall be upon his shoulder: and his name shall be called Wonderful, Counselor, The mighty God, The everlasting Father, The *Prince of Peace*. Of the increase of his government and peace there shall be no end, upon the *throne of David*, and upon *his kingdom*, to order it, and to establish it with judgment and with justice from henceforth even for ever. The zeal of the Lord of hosts will perform this." Words such as Prince, Throne and Kingdom all point directly to Royalty! The inscription above His cross read, "Jesus of Nazareth The King of the Jews" (John 19:19).

The verse's final descriptive phrase states that this royal chariot's midst is paved with love. There is so much that could be said here! The central core of God's kingdom is LOVE. In an earlier scene we learned that the banner over us as believers is love. He loves us. We, in turn, respond by loving Him. Love for each one of us drove Jesus to Calvary where He gave His life so that His sinless blood could wash away our sins. His love for us doesn't give us license to continue in our sin but rather provides a way for us to have our sins washed away, and for us to walk in newness of life.

11 Go forth, O ye daughters of Zion, and behold king Solomon with the crown wherewith his mother crowned him in the day of his espousals, and in the day of the gladness of his heart.

Here's a question for you: how did Mary, the mother of Jesus, crown her son Jesus?

I humbly submit that His Father crowned him with divinity; Mary crowned him with humanity. God manifested in human flesh, conceived in a virgin's womb and carried there, nurtured by her bloodstream, for nine months.

In Hebrews 2:9 we read, "But we see Jesus, who was made a little lower than the angels for the suffering of death." Jesus, the only begotten of the Father, came to earth in a human body for the specific purpose of giving His life for our salvation. The verse doesn't end there, though. It goes on to say, "crowned with glory and honour; that He by the grace of God should taste death for every man." Crowned with thorns in His humanity; crowned with glory and honour in His divinity.

We've watched as the magnificent royal chariot rolled onto the stage. Now a backdrop is raised with a shadowed painting of Calvary. Hebrews 12: 2 states, "Looking unto Jesus the author and finisher of our faith; who for the joy that was set before him (*in the day of the gladness of his heart*), endured the cross, despising the shame, and is set down at the right hand of the throne of God."

Calvary was not a joyous event. It was not a celebration. It was excruciatingly painful, shameful and humiliating for Jesus. On that day, the man Jesus wore a crown of thorns. A crown pressed on his brow because, as a man, He was fulfilling His destiny of crucifixion. His destiny was to be the Saviour of the world. His throne was a rugged cross. The eternal God did not die on that cross. The man, Jesus of Nazareth, shed his sinless blood for us and died a horrible death. The only respite He had from the agony of those hours was His vision of the Church that would be born a few days later, on the Day of Pentecost. That spectacular vision of the Bride to whom He would be espoused gave Him strength to endure the excruciating pain. You and I were in that vision, washed in His blood when we repented, buried in His Name at our baptism, resurrected through His Spirit when we received the gift of the Holy Ghost! The joyful vision of His espoused Bride included millions of individuals from across the globe, from every tribe and nation.

End of Act III, Scene II

Act III, Scene III
Deeper Understanding
Song of Solomon 4:6-8

6 Until the day break, and the shadows flee away, I will get me to the mountain of myrrh; and to the hill of frankincense.

As the curtain rises in chapter four, we see just the two of them, the Shepherd/King and the Bride, having another private moment where beautiful words of loving admiration are spoken. They aren't skipping, dancing or leaping at this time, but rather, they are sharing quiet, intimate secrets. The mood is serious. The Bride is no longer frivolous and carefree; she has reached a level of maturity where her Beloved can share much more significant information with her.

Verse six reinforces the concept we were introduced to in the previous scene: the Shepherd/King revealing to the Believer, His Bride, that between this present moment and the moment of spectacular revelation to the world of who I am there will be a time of darkness, filled with shadows. You will always have hope, He tells His Bride, because eventually the day *will break* and the shadows *will flee away*, but in the meantime, I have a mountain to climb. A mountain of myrrh, a hill of frankincense. I will face suffering, pain, humiliation and death.

Mountains have a prominent place in the ministry of Jesus. We saw him climb a mountain of temptation before He began His earthly ministry. Then we watched him climb a mountain to preach a great sermon. He and his three closest confidantes climbed a mountain where He was transfigured before them. It was in a garden on the side of a mountain where He prayed on that most critical night of His life. He was crucified on Mount Golgotha, and He ascended into Heaven from the Mount of Olives.

In these words of King Solomon there is a sense of purpose and intention: I will get me to the mountain of myrrh, and to the hill of frankincense. I will fulfil the plan. I have made up my mind. No matter the cost, I will do what I was sent into the world to do. As Isaiah penned, "…I have set my face like a flint" (Isaiah 50:7).

Take note that we've shifted from a "bundle" of myrrh that the Believer cradled in an earlier scene to a "mountain" of suffering that Jesus will have to climb. In comparison to the agony He bore on Calvary's mountain, carrying the weight of the sin of the world on his shoulders, any suffering you and I experience in our lives is not a great amount. Any worship that I give, even in those times when I find myself offering a *sacrifice* of praise, is only a small bundle of myrrh when compared to the mountain of myrrh that Jesus was assigned to climb.

7 Thou art all fair, my love; there is no spot in thee.

What is there for the Bride to say when confronted with this reality? Simply this: There is no sign of imperfection in You. Your love is perfect love that has cast out my fear. She doesn't really comprehend why He is suggesting that a time of suffering lies ahead after she so recently had the revelation of His majesty and royalty, but she is committed to Him, her Lover, and what she *does* know is that He will never deceive her or lead her astray. The Bride cannot see the plan ahead clearly but the experiences she has already gone through on this spiritual journey have given her 20/20 vision of the Shepherd/King. There is no imperfection in Him and she can trust Him implicitly.

Pilate echoed the Bride's statement when, after the mock trial of Jesus, he said, "I find no fault in this man." Pilate did not know Jesus in any intimate manner but his assessment of His character was, as the Bride said, *there is no spot in thee.*

The Bride has come a very long way since the first scene of emotional infatuation in Act I! Revelation and understanding have been bestowed upon her as she spends quiet, contemplative hours with the Lover of her soul. The relationship between them has deepened; He has walked with her and talked to her, and has shared deep secrets with her. It's been so important for the Bride not to stop and settle at any stage of this experience; it's been imperative that she continues to listen when He speaks and to follow Him when he leads her forward.

As we pursue Jesus in our own personal, spiritual journey, we must ensure that we never stop and settle down in our experience with Him.

We may struggle in the dark cave of trial, we may have to spend time finding Him again when we have become complacent. But we must keep going forward and keep growing in knowledge, in patience, in commitment. We must never allow ourselves to believe that we have reached the apex of spiritual maturity - there is always more for us to do. We must continue to "press toward the mark" until we reach Heaven.

8 Come with me from Lebanon, my spouse, with me from Lebanon: look from the top of Amana, from the top of Shenir and Hermon, from the lions' dens, from the mountains of the leopards.

Speaking of mountains…The moment of deep soul-baring has passed, and the mood has changed again. In my mind's eye I see the Shepherd/King rising to his feet, His hand outstretched to give assistance to His Bride to stand beside Him. We're not going to wallow here indefinitely with thoughts of the pain and suffering that lies ahead; there's something important that I need to show you. Come with me, I'm taking you on another adventure. We're going to climb some mountains together, and I'm going to give you a vision. A vision that will challenge and energise you. I want you to look from the mountain peaks, to see the spectacular view in every direction. As an afterthought, the Shepherd/King concedes that yes, there *could* be lions and leopards to contend with on the mountainous slopes, but the possibility of meeting dangerous lions and leopards is not enough to deter Him from this next challenge.

In this verse I hear the echo of the Lord's conversation with Abraham many years earlier: "…Lift up now thine eyes, and look from the place where thou are northward, and southward, and eastward, and westward: for all the land which thou seest, to thee will I give it, and to thy seed forever" (Genesis 13:14-15).

As their relationship continues to mature and grow, the Shepherd/King is revealing another facet of His character to His Bride. *I am a man of vision.* I'm not content to sit with you under this shady tree for days on end, revelling in our love for each other. Our relationship is not only about you receiving My blessings. I appreciate your worship. It thrills me to hear you say how perfect I am. But there's more that I expect from you! So much more! There is purpose to your life! I want you to see the possibilities that I have seen. I want to show you the amazing vistas of opportunity that are available to you. My vision is going to become your vision! Let's go to the top of the mountain!

And so, the maturing Believer arrives at the knowledge that this incredible experience she's having is not one that can fit into a small box. It's not meant to be lived out in the confines of a narrow worldview - just You and me. You loving me and me loving You. You meeting my needs. You patting my back and comforting me when I am facing a difficult moment. The Believer is catching a vision of endless possibilities, places to go and sights to see. A vision of purpose to be fulfilled in her life. Mountains to be climbed. Goals to be achieved. Heights to be reached.

I love how Paul expressed this challenge in Philippians 3:12-14. He said, (in the new Georgene Shalm revised version), I haven't reached the top of the mountain yet. But I'm following my leader, hoping to figure out (apprehend) why Jesus Christ apprehended (caught) me. I'm forgetting what went on in my past and I'm reaching into the future. I am pressing, expending energy, straining to reach the prize of the high (mountain top) calling that God has planned for me.

I want to say to you, the reader: Climb out of that small, limited box you've been hiding in! Put on your boots! Grab your gear! Climb the mountain! Expand your vision! Don't settle for a spiritual existence that only involves you being blessed and having your needs met. Move on from that immature stage we learned about in the first act, where the peasant girl was only concerned about where and what she would be fed, and where she would find rest. You're not that immature new believer anymore. Step up and accept the challenge of apprehending God's purpose for your life. Start reaching. Start pressing toward the mark. We believers are destined for great things. We're destined to see and do mighty acts in the Kingdom of God.

In Isaiah 54:2, the prophet advised the people to enlarge the place of their tent, to stretch forth the curtains of their habitation, to spare not, to lengthen their cords and strengthen their stakes. The prophet Ezekiel talked about a river flowing out from under the door of the temple. At first, the waters were shallow, only up to the ankle, and then they gradually deepened until there were waters to swim in. The writer of the Chronicles wrote about a young man named Jabez who prayed, even though his life was disadvantaged, that his coast would be enlarged. Over and over again we are challenged by the Word to catch a vision of greater things. We are challenged to enlarge our tent to include more people, more ethnicities, more cultures. We are challenged to swim into the depths of the flow of the Spirit, where we can see the power of God on display. We are challenged to have our borders enlarged to include people from other belief systems, people whose lifestyles make us uncomfortable, people who desperately need their lives transformed.

Pastor, what's the vision for your church? Missionary, what's the vision for your nation? Youth leader, what's your vision for those teenagers? Sunday School teacher, what's the vision for your class? Parent, what's the vision for your family?

Let's go to the mountain! Let's accept the challenge of catching a vision! Let's climb out of our narrow, confining spaces, throw our arms wide open, take a deep breath and soar to the heights. I can do something for God. I can be someone for God. I can go somewhere for God. I have caught the vision!

End of Act III Scene III

Rise up, My Love, And Come Away

ACT IV

Act IV, Scene I
The Gardener and His Garden
Song of Solomon 4:12-5:1

12 A garden inclosed is my sister, my spouse; a spring shut up, a fountain sealed.

In earlier scenes we have had brief references to seasons and the concept of fruit growing but not yet ripened. Now in this scene we are going to stop and discuss at some length the expectation that the Shepherd/King has for His beloved Bride. That expectation is growth and maturity. From the opening scene we have been considering the Bride's journey from being a new and somewhat naive convert through various stages of becoming a strong, mature, fruitful Believer. Sadly, many individuals come to the Lord, have a wonderful experience of salvation, but then get stuck on that initial level of seeking blessings and having their needs met, never learning how to walk with God and how to develop the fruit of the Spirit. I don't want to be that person; as Paul said, I want to *know* Him in the power of His resurrection and the fellowship of His suffering. So let's stop here for a while and talk about being fruitful Believers.

It is quite apparent in the Word that our Lord loves gardens. When God first created the world, he placed Adam and Eve in a garden. Jesus made a habit of praying with His disciples in the Garden of Gethsemane, and of course, that's where He prayed the most crucial prayer of His life. He was buried in a garden tomb, and was even mistaken by Mary to be the gardener!

Now in this passage King Solomon compares His beloved Bride to a garden. A place of beauty, growth and fruitfulness.

I must confess that in my life I have not had much success as a gardener. As a youngster living in Pembroke, Ontario, a sweet little lady in our church kindly allotted me a corner in her backyard where I enthusiastically planted pumpkin and squash seeds one summer. Sadly, my enthusiasm quickly waned when I realised I would have to walk up the road to her house almost daily and spend time weeding my little pumpkin patch.

I had more success when my father bought me a packet of morning glory seeds to plant around an old, disused "out-house" at the far end of our church property in Pembroke. After an indoor bathroom had been installed in the parsonage, my friends and I were allowed to turn that "out-house" into a clubhouse. (Don't even ask!). That summer the old weather-beaten shed blazed in magnificent shades of bright pink and mauve as the morning glory blossoms wound their way up its outer walls. Sadly for the out-house, though, by the next summer, my interests had moved on to tadpoles and chipmunks.

Thankfully, our Lord's reputation as a loving Gardener is much stronger than mine!

As mentioned earlier, a garden is a place of beauty, peace and growth, whether it is a flower garden or a vegetable patch. A garden is not the same as a farm; its purpose is not mass production. Flower gardens are for pleasure; vegetable gardens are for personal use, and perhaps to be shared with neighbours if you have a bumper crop of zucchini and green peppers. If there are fruit trees in your garden, they will provide delicious nourishment as well as beauty, fragrance and shade.

Our new Believer and Bride, the beautiful peasant girl, has slowly but surely transitioned from someone whose eyes are continually taking in all the delights of this new experience without much personal responsibility, to an individual who is "putting down roots", a person who has become productive. Her life gives great pleasure to her much-loved Shepherd/King.

We are created and designed to bring pleasure to the Master Gardener. He delights in seeing our growth and development as we mature in our walk with Him, as we put our roots into the Word, as we develop Christian character, and as the fruit of the Spirit is manifested in our daily living.

Weeding and pruning is required in any garden, and the result of that labour will be more beauty and more production. The goal of any gardener is always growth. Bare dirt with seeds buried in it does not provide much nourishment or beauty. The intention for those seeds is for them to break out of their shell and to begin to grow. At first only a little green shoot will be seen. If growth stops at that point, the seed has been wasted. No gardener or farmer anywhere in the world is satisfied with tiny green shoots breaking through the soil. Every gardener's expectation is growth. Every farmer's expectation is growth.

Our heavenly Gardener is no exception. He is looking for progress in our spiritual walk with God. He's not satisfied for us to remain immature, like little green shoots barely peeking out from the surrounding dirt. Remember how unhappy Jesus was with the fig tree that only had leaves?

This concept of required growth is a recurring one in the New Testament.

In Colossians 1:9, The Apostle Paul wrote, "For this cause we also, since the day we heard it, do not cease to pray for you, and to desire that ye might be filled with the knowledge of his will in all wisdom and spiritual understanding." In other words, Paul told the Colossian believers that growth and maturity was an expectation.

John 12:24 tells us that Jesus declared, "Verily, verily, I say unto you, Except a corn of wheat fall into the ground and die, it abideth alone: but if it die, it bringeth forth much fruit."

The seed pod must die and decay so that new life can spring forth. *That is the expectation for every seed that is planted.*

I love the promise in Psalm 72:16, "There shall be an handful of corn in the earth upon the top of the mountains; the fruit thereof shall shake like Lebanon: and they of the city shall flourish like grass of the earth." We believers are that handful of corn. Not seeds that are content to stay wrapped up in their safe, little pod, totally unproductive, but seeds that have accepted the challenge of the mountain, with the potential to flourish and become very powerful.

God's expectation for every believer is that we will become mature, productive, fruit-bearing branches nourished by the Vine.

In John 15:1-8 Jesus gave some very clear teaching on His expectation that His disciples would be fruitful. He told them that He was the vine, and that His Father was the husbandman (the caretaker of the orchard). Each one of them was a branch growing out of the main vine, and if they did not bear fruit, they would be "taken away". If buds did appear on the branch, they needed to be aware that the husbandman would purge, or prune the branch, so that the fruit would have the best possible environment in which to ripen into maturity. Pruning is not especially comfortable, but it is a necessary process in order to have healthy fruit.

Believers are not expected to produce fruit on their own, but as we stay attached to the Vine, growth will happen organically. "Abide in Me," Jesus said. In other words, live in my presence. Merely visiting once in a while on a Sunday morning or a Wednesday night Bible study is not the same as abiding. But the wonderful promise to each one of us is, if we will abide in Him, we will bring forth much fruit.

The Shepherd/King described His Beloved as an inclosed garden. He didn't specify what was growing in the garden, but I have some ideas.

Galatians 5:22-23 describes the fruit of the Spirit. As we allow the Spirit to do some weeding and pruning in our hearts and lives, the result will be very beautiful: love, joy, peace, longsuffering, gentleness, goodness, faith, meekness and temperance will begin to grow. The growth doesn't happen overnight, as the Believer will learn as she surrenders to the gardener's skill, but over time His handiwork will be clearly seen in our lives.

The Apostle Peter added his insight to Paul's words in Galatians. In II Peter 1:5-8, he advises us to add virtue to our faith, and once virtue is showing healthy growth, then add knowledge to your garden. After knowledge comes temperance, then patience, followed by godliness. No garden is complete without a border of brotherly kindness which blends readily with charity. Peter sums it all up for us by saying, "If these things be in you, and abound, they make you that you shall neither be barren nor unfruitful in the knowledge of our Lord Jesus Christ." He ended his second letter with the admonition to "grow in grace, and in the knowledge of our Lord and Saviour." (II Peter 3:18).

Peter himself was an iconic example of the growth he was writing about. In our early acquaintance with Simon Peter, we saw him as an impetuous, outspoken fisherman. As Jesus gathered several young men to be his disciples, Peter was often the spokesperson whenever there was a disagreement. His betrayal of Jesus showed the weakness of his character. But under the tutelage of the Holy Spirit, Peter became one of the great apostles of the early church. He boldly stepped onto the world's stage on the Day of Pentecost to preach the first Gospel message. He was the first one to share that Gospel message with Gentiles. He slipped up and had to be corrected by Paul on one occasion, part of the growth process, but went on to be a strong leader.

In this relationship of the Believer/Bride and the Shepherd/King, and in our relationship with Jesus, growth is an expectation. As we follow Jesus in this spiritual journey, there is little tolerance for unproductive disciples, or for those who do not mature in their spiritual understanding.

Notice that the poet said this garden was *inclosed*. A walled garden. Protected. Oh, the safety and assurance we find as we entrust our lives to the Master Gardener! His precious blood provides a wall of safety against the attacks of the enemy of our soul. The angel of the Lord encamps round about them that fear him, and delivers them (Psalm 34:7). The parapets of righteousness and holiness that we construct around our homes and lives, as commanded in Deuteronomy 22:8, protect us from fatal spiritual mistakes, and provide a strong deterrent against temptation. Those kinds of walls are very necessary for every believer.

However, walls built by pride, self-righteousness, culture, abuse, past hurts, betrayal, failure, disappointment, self-doubt, criticism, offence, unforgiveness, bitterness, arrogance, even personality, have a very negative aspect to them *if we've built them ourselves*. One by one, over an extended period of time, the bricks are placed on top of each other until we have completely walled ourselves in. If that is the situation you find yourself in, please allow the Master Builder, Jesus, to remove those walls from your life and to build in their place His specially designed walls of love and protection.

The King went on to say that this Bride of His was not only a garden full of beauty and fruit to be shared, but she was also a spring that had been shut up and a fountain that had been sealed.

This speaks to me about potential that has been stifled.

A spring flows *naturally*. It bubbles up through the ground close to a pathway, or chisels its way through rock to surprise mountain climbers. Spring water is pure and cool and provides delicious refreshment to those who are thirsty. This "spring" refers to the natural abilities, talents and circumstances with or into which the Bride was born. We don't choose our place of birth, our birth family, our ethnicity - those are all chosen for us naturally. We don't decide whether we'll have artistic ability, or musical ability. We don't select a personality type for ourselves. Clearly, those things can be enhanced and influenced by experience and practice, but often those natural traits become apparent just a few months after a baby is born.

Sadly, this spring is described as "shut up." Debris, fallen leaves, or items of trash, have collected over time at the mouth of the spring and blocked its flow. This didn't necessarily occur by design but as a result of lack of care, neglect, and the passage of time.

For some reason, the Bride is not using these natural abilities and circumstances to full advantage, perhaps because she's been criticised or hurt, perhaps because there's been a lack of opportunity, or perhaps because her personality inhibits her. Whatever the reason, help is needed to remove the hindrances so the spring can flow freely again.

A fountain, on the other hand, is not natural. No fountain in a town square got there by itself! Fountains are designed and built deliberately, and are connected on purpose to a source of water. This represents deliberate decisions we've taken concerning our education, financial investments and our career, opportunities we've taken advantage of when they were presented to us, and the choice we've made about a life partner.

The poet tells us that the fountain was "sealed", which was a deliberate and conscious act. Whether the sealing was done by an outsider or by the Bride herself, the fountain is not functioning as intended, and requires someone to come and remove the seal.

Let's go back to that scene again in Luke 4:18 where Jesus announced in the Nazareth synagogue that through the anointing that was upon Him, the poor would have the gospel preached to them, broken hearts would be healed, captives would be set free, blind eyes would be opened, and those who were bruised would be set free. It's not His will for His Bride to struggle with a broken heart or a bruised spirit. Jesus wants us to be able to navigate through the world with clear vision. His Holy Spirit is the agent that can remove any blockage at the mouth of the spring, and to break the seal that has stopped the flow of the fountain. Momentarily, that process may cause discomfort to our hearts and spirits, but oh, how wonderful to be restored to wholeness again by His Holy Spirit!

The promise found in Isaiah 58:11 speaks to each one of us, "And the Lord shall guide thee continually, and satisfy thy soul in drought, and make fat thy bones: and thou shalt be like a watered garden, and like a spring of water, whose waters fail not."

End of Act IV, Scene I

Act IV, Scene II
The Gardener and His Garden, continued
Song of Solomon 4:13-16

13 - 14 Thy plants are an orchard of pomegranates, with pleasant fruits; camphir, with spikenard, spikenard and saffron; calamus and cinnamon, with all trees of frankincense; myrrh and aloes, with all the chief spices.

The garden is in full bloom now. Growth has taken place that can minister to other people, an entire orchard, in fact! It's a beautiful place filled with the scents of camphir, spikenard, saffron, cinnamon, frankincense, myrrh, aloes, and all the chief spices. Some of these aromatic plants were ingredients in the anointing oil used in the Tabernacle; others represent the trials and tests of life, and of course, spikenard represents our sacrificial worship. The growth that is taking place is multi-faceted and gives the Master Gardener great pleasure.

16 Awake, O north wind; and come, thou south; blow upon my garden, that the spices thereof may flow out.

Let my beloved come into his garden, and eat his pleasant fruits.

The Bride has come to the realisation that there is more required of her than simply pleasing her Beloved. Although pleasing her Beloved *is* a priority, she understands that there are people on the other side of the wall for whom the fragrance of her garden would be a great blessing. And so she invites the wind from the north and from the south to blow upon her garden, which will cause the beautiful scents to flow out and over the wall.

I lived in Pakistan for thirty years. Each January, our gardener would install vertical rows of string along our boundary wall, and then he would plant some tiny round seeds that were quite unimpressive as far as size goes, along the base of the wall. The winter rains fell and before long, tiny green shoots would break through the soil. At this stage of growth there wasn't much to get excited about, really. Soon, though, the little shoots became vines that wound their way up the strings. And then, before too long, lovely flowers, which were called "sweet peas", appeared on the vines. Pink, purple, blue, mauve, yellow, and white blossoms all grew together, a veritable feast for the eyes. And their fragrance! A few tiny flowers in a vase filled our home with their perfume.

I used to love walking in our neighbourhood during those spring days, because ours wasn't the only house whose gardener had planted sweet peas. Along every street and lane, from behind the boundary walls of each home, wafted the intoxicating scent of those blossoms.

Although walls and locked gates kept the residents of those homes safe from intruders, it was impossible for them to stop the fragrance of their garden escaping over the wall whenever a slight breeze blew.

There are times in our lives when the wind begins to blow. It may be a north wind bringing with it the rain of illness or the loss of a job. It may be the wind of misunderstanding between family members. Or it could be the refreshing south wind of blessing and peace. Whichever wind blows in our direction, an opportunity is created for the fruit of the Spirit that's been nurtured by the Gardener's hand to flow out to bless others. The aroma of longsuffering when a difficult situation is not resolved in our favour. The perfume of love when faced with difficult personalities. The fragrance of meekness when an apology is necessary. The scent of joy when a blessing is shared with others.

The Apostle Paul wrote in his second epistle to the church in Corinth, "For we are unto God a sweet savour of Christ, in them that are saved, and in them that perish" (II Corinthians 2:15). Each one of us, as believers, develops, over time, a fragrance or an aroma as Jesus works in the gardens of our hearts, weeding out hindrances to our growth and nurturing the soil so the precious seeds of the Word grow and flourish with beauty. That perfume, rising from our lives up to God, gives Him great pleasure. We are evidence to Him that His plan, set in motion from the very foundation of the world, has been successful.

The Believer has grown and matured through her recent experiences on her spiritual journey. She had exerted the energy required to climb to the top of the mountain where visions of possibility were shared with her by the Shepherd/King. No longer constantly needing encouragement and motivation for herself, she is becoming aware of others' needs, and how she can be a blessing to others rather than just receiving blessings.

The pattern has been established for us. We begin our walk with God as "babes in Christ," who are immature and needy. Gradually each one of us changes as we walk through valleys, as we go up and down those stairs in the caves, as we respond to the Shepherd/King's encouragement to climb the mountain and obtain a new vision. If you've known the Lord for some time but you still find yourself wavering, struggling, always needing assurance and assistance and never acknowledging the requirements of others who need ministering to, perhaps you need to take time to evaluate your experience. We don't want the Gardener to be disappointed in us!

End of Act IV, Scene II

Rise up, My Love,
And Come Away

ACT V

Act V, Scene I
Complacency
Song of Solomon 5: 2-7

2 I sleep, but my heart waketh: it is the voice of my beloved that knocketh, saying, Open to me, my sister, my love, my dove, my undefiled: for my head is filled with dew, and my locks with the drops of the night.

As the curtain rises on this fifth act, the first thing we notice is that the backdrop, previously painted with fluffy clouds, a brightly shining sun, mountain-top vistas, and peaceful gardens, is now a dismal pattern of greys mixed with black. Immediately our senses are piqued: an atmosphere of sadness creeps stealthily across the audience.

The Believer, no longer considered to be a "new" believer but one who has had life-changing experiences with the Shepherd/King and who has grown into maturity, with newly acquired vision and understanding of her required contributions, is blissfully asleep. Sweet dreams! She has found a level of comfort in her spiritual experience. Even while asleep, though, she is aware of her Lover nearby. His presence is unmistakeable; his voice easily recognisable. Her heart immediately responds ~ I know that voice! I've heard Him speak precious words of love to me.

The Voice tells her she is loved and pure. Mmmm ~ that's what she likes to hear! But what is this He is asking her to do? He wants her to get up from her comfortable, cozy resting place and open the door? Doesn't He know how late it is? Doesn't He know how exhausted she is? The two of them have been so busy lately, she really needs her rest. This interruption isn't exactly what she was expecting.

3 I have put off my coat; how shall I put it on? I have washed my feet; how shall I defile them?

Now a new phase in their relationship begins: excuses!

With every challenge the Believer has faced until now, her response has always been to take her Lover's hand and follow Him. But for some reason, in this scene she's not quite as enthusiastic as she was before. She's already made so much progress! Surely, she deserves a break? She explains that it's not convenient for her to get up and open the door. Yes, she knows He always has something wonderful to show her or to share with her, but, she's *really* comfortable here. She's not exactly in "church mode". She's washed her feet (shades of self-righteousness!), surely, He doesn't expect her to get them dirty, does He?

How many believers come this far in their relationship with Jesus, only to settle down into a comfortable spot (rut) from which they really would rather not be disturbed? I've been busy climbing mountains, they say. I've been working in my garden. I have made great progress in my walk with God. You should have seen me when I first got saved! I really feel that I deserve to take a break once in a while! Sure, I'll show up for Sunday morning, but it's a bit of a stretch to expect me at prayer meeting on Saturday night! Me, teach Sunday School? Me, teach a Bible study? I've been through quite a lot recently; I really need some "me-time". I'd like to be left alone, if You don't mind.

Does any of that sound familiar? Any of you reading this identify with such feelings?

The Believer has become *complacent*, and as a result, is on the fast track to calamity. This is such a dangerous place for the Believer in which to find herself. Apathy oozes out of every pore.

The Believer will never know what her Lover was going to share with her that night, what revelation He had prepared, what blessings He was bringing with Him. She'll never know what she missed, because "me-time" took priority over "us-time".

4 My beloved put in his hand by the hole of the door, and my bowels were moved for him.

How desperately the Shepherd/King wanted to spend time with her! She heard the rattle of the doorknob as He tried to reach in and open the door. It was locked from the inside - she was the only one who could open it. Her innermost being responded to his attempts to draw her out of her comfort zone. She knew she should get up from her resting place. The Spirit was convicting her. That stirring she was feeling required action on her part.

> *5 I rose up to open to my beloved; and my hands dropped with myrrh, and my fingers with sweet smelling myrrh, upon the handles of the lock.*

She struggles and finally gives in: okay, okay, I'm *coming*! She's decided to make the effort, albeit reluctantly. As she reaches to open the door, the lingering effects of His sweet presence at the door transfer to her hands. It's an effect that's familiar to her. He had been so close!

But what she hasn't realised is that, at this point in her relationship with the Shepherd/King, the stakes are much higher, the demands and the expectations are greater than they were at the beginning. He is not quite as tolerant with her now as He was when she was a new believer. Rather than patiently waiting for her to respond to His voice, He withdraws. Moves on.

> *6 I opened to my beloved: but my beloved had withdrawn himself, and was gone: my soul failed when he spake: I sought him, but I could not find him; I called him, but he gave me no answer.*

Bad timing. Missed opportunities. If only. Too late. The road to hell is paved with good intentions. The cliches can roll off my tongue so easily, but those cheap words mask one tragedy after another, tragedies that will be revealed in eternity, when it will be, literally, too late!

The Bride didn't necessarily want to end the relationship. She was still in love with her Shepherd/King. Her heart still leapt within her when she heard her Lover's voice. But she was just *so* tired! A few more minutes curled up under the duvet isn't going to hurt anybody, is it?

I wonder how many times the Lord Jesus came to my door and found me too complacent to get up and let Him in? What revelations might I have discovered in His Word? What understanding might I have gained? What answers to prayer may have been granted? How many souls might have been delivered?

And so, the Believer puts on her robe and her slippers and shuffles to the door, only to discover that her Beloved has withdrawn Himself. He gave up waiting for her. He doesn't scold her or put pressure on her. He simply withdraws. She switches on the verandah light to have a look around. Well, I know that He was here a minute ago, she thinks to herself. Where could He have gone? I'll just take a quick walk up the driveway and call His name. But sadly, there's no response when she calls. It is at this juncture she decides it would be a good idea for her to get dressed and go looking for Him.

King Solomon made an interesting choice of words when he said that the Beloved had "withdrawn himself." He didn't simply walk away, but He intentionally slipped out of her environment. He was not totally abandoning the Believer, but was giving her an opportunity to learn the value of His presence by allowing her to experience moments without it. It wouldn't be long before the comprehension would dawn that nothing could ever compensate for the lack of His presence in her life.

Thankfully, the Believer eventually made the correct decision. She got up from her place of ease, put on her shoes and did whatever was necessary to insure He was beside her again!

End of Act V, Scene I

Act V, Scene II
Calamity
Song of Solomon 5:7-8

7 The watchmen that went about the city found me, they smote me, they wounded me; the keepers of the walls took away my veil from me.

Oh, how I wish we could skip over this scene! It has tragedy written all over it.

The curtain rises and we see the Believer, disheveled, frantic, running a few steps in one direction and then a few steps in the opposite direction, with a look of panic on her face. It's the middle of the night so the stage has been darkened accordingly. Her complacency has landed her in a very unfortunate situation. Instead of walking hand-in-hand with her Beloved as He reveals to her a deeper revelation of His person, which was His intention when he so insistently knocked on her door, she is alone, desperately trying to locate His presence.

And then footsteps are heard behind her. Ah, relief! Help is on the way. These men will surely be able to direct me in the right way.

Watchmen. Keepers of the walls. Men who watch. Men who guard. Men who have the very important responsibility of keeping believers safe. How thankful we should be for those countless watchmen who stand guard through the long dark nights, sleepless nights for them because their assignment requires constant vigilance, constant awareness of danger, and constant awareness of approaching enemies. Their responsibility is to raise their voice against enemies sneaking surreptitiously through the city gates, waiting for an opportunity to pounce on unfortunate, unsuspecting prey.

The prophet Isaiah wrote about trustworthy watchmen who stand faithfully at their post: "Watchman, what of the night? Watchman, what of the night?" The watchman said, "The morning cometh (for those of us who know the Lord) and also the night (for those who have rejected Him)" Isaiah 21:11-12. Those are the kind of watchmen we need in our lives and leading our churches!

Sadly, the footsteps the Believer heard on this occasion belonged to a small minority of rogue watchmen. Watchmen who used their position to punish those who had lost their way rather than rescue them. Watchmen who smote her for being out alone on the streets at night, totally misinterpreting her situation. Rather than binding up the wounds she'd gotten as she stumbled in the darkness they exacerbated those wounds. They exposed her, shamed and humiliated her. Yes, she had made a terrible error of judgment when she rejected her Beloved's invitation, but it was a *mistake,* not a reflection of her love for the Shepherd/King. She didn't deserve their treatment of her in that moment of weakness.

Many of us have encountered this kind of watchman on our spiritual journey. Men and women who had been commissioned to care for our souls but abused their power to the detriment of those who were seeking direction from them. Thankfully, they are few and far between, but there are enough of them to deserve a place in our Believer's story. Oh, the hurt and betrayal these rogue watchmen leave in their wake!

Watchmen, you better watch yourselves while you're watching others! Your assignment is to guard, to protect, to direct, and to ensure safety for the inhabitants of your city. When a Believer makes a mistake, you need to be available to direct them back onto the path of life. You need to ensure they get reconnected to the Shepherd/King.

8 I charge you, O daughters of Jerusalem, if ye find my beloved, that ye tell him, that I am sick of love.

A crowd of other believers has gathered at the scene, as always happens when something unusual occurs. Everyone has an opinion or an observation. The Believer lifts her head, too weary and battered to rise to her feet. I am overwhelmed, she states. This journey is much more difficult than I expected. I thought we would always be leaping over mountains, smelling beautiful flowers, gazing at spectacular vistas from the mountaintop. I didn't anticipate that He would ask me to get up in the middle of the night to follow Him! I'm exhausted. I need rehabilitation. I need ointment for my wounds. I need a refreshing drink. This spiritual journey I've been on has definitely been exhilarating, but I am worn out. If this is "love", then I'm over it!

And so, we see the Believer, crumpled in a heap on the stage floor, bleeding, heartbroken and desperately in need of an outstretched hand to help her get back on her feet. This terrible experience has been nothing but calamity for her.

Or has it? Could it be that she has had the wake-up call of all wake-up calls? Could it be that these recent hours of fear and betrayal have brought her to a place where she "gets it", where she understands just how precious this relationship with the Shepherd/King is to her?

9 What is thy beloved more than another beloved, O thou fairest among women? What is thy beloved more than another beloved, that thou dost so charge us?

The daughters of Jerusalem, those curious, uncommitted believers standing on the edge of the crowd, ask her: What is so special about this man, that you've been willing to go through so many difficult times, and face so many challenges just to be with Him? Has it really been worth it? Look at you, scarred from the trials you've encountered along the way, battered, bruised and discouraged. Can you really tell us that the struggle has been worth it?

10 - 16 My beloved is white and ruddy, the chiefest among ten thousand. His head is as the most fine gold, his locks are bushy, and black as a raven. His eyes are as the eyes of doves by the rivers of waters, washed with milk, and fitly set. His cheeks are as a bed of spices, as sweet flowers: his lips like lilies, dropping sweet smelling myrrh. His hands are as gold rings set with the beryl: his belly is as bright ivory overlaid with sapphires. His legs are as pillars of marble, set upon sockets of fine gold: his countenance is as Lebanon, excellent as the cedars. His mouth is most sweet: yea, he is altogether lovely. This is my beloved, and this is my friend, O daughters of Jerusalem.

The probing questions of the daughters of Jerusalem force the Believer to assess the situation. On one hand, she has definitely gone through some very difficult circumstances in her pursuit of the Shepherd/King. No one can ever deny that. On the other hand, she realises beyond any doubt that this relationship that she could never have even imagined in the not-so-distant past is definitely worth whatever she has to go through. The trying times have revealed to her the value of His love. Thus, when asked what makes this relationship better than any other, the Believer's response is, how much time do you have? Let me tell you about the Shepherd/King! Let me explain to you all the reasons why I fell in love with Him!

There's so much to tell you! He is the chiefest among ten thousand! He has an aura of power, but such kind and tender eyes! His hands hold divinity in their grasp, but are gentle enough for a child to sense their comfort. He has so much strength! He is so dependable! And He speaks the most wonderful truths into my heart!

Actually, now that I think about it, He is *altogether* lovely. I can find no fault in Him!

At this point in King Solomon's story, a very subtle shift has just taken place. Up until now, the Believer/Bride has been focused on herself, what she will eat, where she will rest, what she is feeling, and whether she is comfortable or not. Being chosen by such a handsome stranger and led on so many different adventures has been absolutely exhilarating. His warm presence as He wraps her in His love has been such a wonderful experience for her, a plain peasant girl.

But after surviving the suffering and humiliation of this recent encounter, the emphasis changes. The Shepherd/King, her beloved Bridegroom, becomes the focus. She has become totally committed to Him. From now on, it's going to be all about Him. I am COMMITTED to following Him. If I have to get up from my comfortable place of rest in the middle of the night to follow Him, that's what I'll do. I'm never again going to take the risk of losing His presence in my life. He is altogether lovely, and there is nothing on offer anywhere in the world that would tempt me away from Him.

I've known precious saints of God who have suffered terrible losses in their lives, others who have been desperately wounded and betrayed. From a natural perspective, bitterness would be a legitimate response to the trials they have faced. Instead, when I hear them speak, their conversation is about the faithfulness of God, about His goodness, and His rich blessings in their lives. Their testimony is always an encouragement to others. Their spirit is sweet. They have committed their lives to the Lord Jesus. They aren't tempted to choose other priorities for their lives. Whatever comes my way, they can be heard to say, I'm going to follow Jesus. I'm going to serve Him with all of my strength. Like the Believer in the Song of Solomon, these saints have learned the priceless value of a relationship with Jesus through times of hardship and deep trials. If you asked them, they would tell you that Jesus is altogether lovely, that there is no fault in Him.

6:2 My beloved is gone down into his garden, to the beds of spices, to feed in the gardens, and to gather lilies.

As the Bride testifies of the wonders of her Lover, Shepherd and King, the defeat that she thought was writing the last few lines of her story is suddenly overcome by a new surge of strength and resolve. She is on her feet again. She is looking at calamity in her rear-view mirror! She has made a decision: I'm going to find Him. I know where He'll be - in His favourite place: His garden, where He will be enjoying the pungent aroma of the spice beds, and the heady perfume of his lilies.

Take note that the Shepherd/King was not in panic mode concerning His precious Bride who was going through a terrible ordeal at that moment. He was not running hither and thither, looking for her. Instead, He calmly went to His garden, because His favourite place is the place where growth occurs, to wait for her. He had invested so much into her life that he had confidence she would survive and that she would find Him again.

That's a valuable lesson for each one of us. We all make mistakes, we all fail. (Not mentioning any names, but her initials could be GS!) Some of us fail miserably and make a total mess of things! We all go through difficult times when we don't react as positively as we should. In those moments of weakness, the devil can sneak up on us and whisper malevolently in our ear that we might as well give up because there's no way back. Don't listen to him! Some of us have had to be shaken out of our complacency by tragedy and deep sorrow. But our Lord and Saviour continues to love us, and He allows the circumstances and situations we face to bring us to a realisation that, above everything else, we desperately need Him in our lives. He never shifts into panic mode. But be very sure that when you turn up at the garden where He's been patiently waiting, He will welcome you with wide open arms!

As the curtain drops on this scene that could have had defeat written all over it, a voice can be heard singing a song of victory:

Micah 7:8 Rejoice not against me, O mine enemy: when I fall, I shall arise; when I sit in darkness, the Lord shall be a light unto me.

End of Act V, Scene II

Rise up, My Love,
And Come Away

ACT VI

Act VI, Scene I
The Lover's Perspective of the Believer
Song of Solomon 6:4-11, 7:1

4 Thou are beautiful, O my love, as Tirzah, comely as Jerusalem, terrible as an army with banners.

After all the commotion and confusion of the previous act, things seem to have settled down somewhat as the house lights dim and the curtain rises again for this first scene of the final act. Each cast member has taken a deep breath. All evidence of the struggle the Believer recently went through has been removed, and a peaceful atmosphere has replaced the distraught mood.

The Shepherd/King looks adoringly at the Believer/Bride who is now a survivor and who is totally committed to Him. His description of her has three very significant aspects.

Firstly, He states that she is as beautiful as Tirzah. The city of Tirzah was the northern capital of Israel for many years. Apparently, the city's location was very appealing, because during the time of the Judges and the Kingdom, several battles were fought over it. In

Hebrew, Tirzah means "pleasing". Another source said, when the name Tirzah was given to a female child, it meant "she is my delight." How fitting!

Secondly, The Shepherd/King declares that His Bride is as comely as Jerusalem. Jerusalem, the city loved by so many throughout the ages! The city of King David, Solomon's father. The Psalmist wrote, "Great is the Lord, and greatly to be praised in the city of our God, in the mountain of his holiness. Beautiful for situation, the joy of the whole earth, is mount Zion, on the sides of the north, the city of the great King" (Psalm 48:1-2). Could Solomon have chosen any other comparison that would be as significant to him as this one?

Thirdly, we are told that the Bride is as terrible as an army with banners. This is the comparison that gives me goosebumps! We've recently seen the Believer in a scene where she had learned through a very difficult experience how absolutely essential it is to be sensitive to her Lover's voice, and to move quickly when He speaks. If you conversed with the Bride immediately following that episode, she would probably tell you that she felt defeated and ashamed, very weak and vulnerable, the very opposite of a victorious army. What great insight this comparison gives us into God's perspective of our trials and tribulations. *She* felt defeated, but because she had survived the distress and abuse, The Lover of her soul saw her as a mighty warrior, an army prepared to go into battle. He describes her as "terrible as an army with banners." We as believers may perceive our struggles as the devil's attack, trying to pull us down, while the Lord Jesus sees those same struggles as a means for us to be spiritually promoted to a much higher level.

Terrible is connected to terror. (I know you know that, but I needed to make the point.) As an experienced survivor, she is now capable of striking absolute terror in the heart of the enemy. Notice He does not describe this much more experienced believer as a mere single soldier. She is equivalent to an army with banners, marching with confidence into the battle. The Bride has learned how to pray effectively. She has learned how to use the weapons of warfare at her disposal. She knows how to use the Word of God to defeat the enemy when he attacks her with his discouraging lies.

Armies that are at ease do not wave their banners. Their banners, or *standards*, are for times of *battle*. Isaiah 59:19 declares, "…When the enemy shall come in like a flood, the Spirit of the Lord shall lift up a standard against him." When the enemy attacks, the Spirit of the Lord that is resident within the bosom of the Believer, announces, "We are not going to lie down and let the enemy walk all over us; we're going into battle!" Faithful Believer, when you are on your knees in your prayer closet, you may see yourself as small and insignificant, but God sees you as a mighty army, coming against the enemy of His Kingdom.

Armies have weapons. They don't usually fight with their fists. The weapons of our warfare are not carnal, but are MIGHTY THROUGH GOD to the pulling down of strongholds (II Corinthians 10:4). He has armed us with the power of His precious blood. He has commanded us to use the Word, the Sword of the Spirit, as an offensive weapon. He has filled us with His Spirit, the promise of power. Don't see yourself ever again as a wimp or a loser! That's not how God sees you and that's not how the devil sees you. You have mighty weapons in your arsenal. The power that a praying saint of God has is mind-blowing!

10 Who is she that looketh forth as the morning, fair as the moon, clear as the sun, and terrible as an army with banners?

I don't know too many things in life that are more faithful than the morning. Every night as the sun sets, you can know with absolute assurance that, in a few hours' time, it will come up again. It doesn't matter what difficult situation you find yourself in during the night, the sun is going to rise. Whether there's a war, or a pandemic, or an earthquake, or a plane crash, or a tsunami - the sun is going to rise in the morning and it's going to set in the evening. You can depend on it. The Shepherd/King compared His mature, battle-scarred Beloved to the arrival of the morning. Faithful. Consistent. Dependable.

He then said that the Believer is fair as the moon. The moon is not a source of light, but is rather a *reflection* of light. We believers reflect the glory of God in our lives. The moon goes through phases, not always visible to us in fullness, but is sometimes just a tiny sliver of light showing in the sky. Always there but not always clearly visible. Our lives can be like that, going through phases…times where we are living in fullness and times when we feel we are hanging on by our fingernails. But, whatever "phase" you find yourself in, you're there, in your place, reflecting the glory of God in your life. Fair as the moon.

In your walk with God, be faithful. Be that one in the congregation that the pastor can depend on. Be that one your family can depend on. Be that one your employer can depend on. Be that one Jesus can depend on. Be faithful!

Finally, there's that phrase again that I love! Who is she that is *terrible as an army with banners*? It's a rhetorical question - we all already know the answer. It's ME! It's YOU! I've been through some battles; I've got scars to prove it and so have you. But the battles didn't defeat us - they promoted us to the level of mighty, experienced warriors. Warriors that are so skilled with their weapons that they can be compared to an entire army. When the devil sees you coming, he doesn't see an individual; he sees an army marching toward him and he absolutely quakes with fear!

11 I went down into the garden of nuts to see the fruits of the valley, and to see whether the vine flourished and the pomegranates budded.

It would have made things so much easier for me as I write this devotional if King Solomon had written, "I went down into the walnut grove…" No one, least of all me, would've batted an eyelash! I don't really think Solomon intended to be amusing or ironic when he wrote these lines, but I'm sure there are some who hide a tiny grin behind their hand when they read this verse! A little comic relief never hurt anybody! If we're all going to be classified as "nuts", I am identifying as an almond! Almonds are good for the heart!

> *13 Return, return, O Shulamite; return, return, that we may look upon thee. What will ye see in the Shulamite? As it were the company of two armies.*

Suddenly some strange voices interrupt the Shepherd/King's monologue. They are voices from the past calling the Believer. Voices from those who knew the Believer when she was simply a peasant, a sun-burned labourer in the vineyard. They don't see her as a beautiful bride, but only as the person she was at the beginning of her story. These are the voices of those who would try to discourage you, to pull you back from your walk with God. Voices from acquaintances who have never fully committed to Jesus and who have settled for a shallow, immature, Sunday-morning only relationship with Him. Aren't we all familiar with these voices in our heads? With sarcasm they say, who exactly do you think you are?

Where do you think you are going? Come on back, we miss you. We haven't seen you for ages. Let's meet for coffee and hang out for a while. Let's have some good fellowship!

Those who don't know the Lord, and, sadly, even some immature believers, are uncomfortable with people who make up their minds to go places in God that are deeper and higher than the "norm". Return,

return, they cry. Don't get too spiritual. Don't go overboard! Remember one aspect of the fruit of the Spirit is temperance. Keep some balance in your life. You see visions? Really? You see angels? *Really?* Be careful - you're going to be so heavenly minded you'll be no earthly good!

Don't listen to those negative voices! Don't let them discourage you and distract you from your focus. Listen to your Saviour's voice. His voice says, Come away with me! I have SO MUCH to show you!

With a look of contempt on their faces, these "old friends" now turn to the Shepherd/King and ask a sarcastic question: "What do you see in this Shulamite?" The inference is that she is unworthy of the Shepherd/King's love. She's just a peasant girl, after all. She does manual labour in a vineyard, for goodness sake! She has nothing to offer You. She's not anything special - just another lily among thousands of lilies in the valley. Why would You even look at her twice?

The Lover/Shepherd/King responds to their question. I love His answer. He tells them, I don't see what you see. I don't see a sun-burned peasant girl. I don't see someone ordinary or unworthy of my love. I see someone who is strong, someone who has made amazing progress in her journey with me. I see a mature Believer, who has been through some difficult situations, has faced mountains in her life but has just kept moving forward. She hasn't given up. To sum it up for you, I see, as it were, the company of *two* armies.

What would be a suitable comeback for a statement like that? Exactly. There is no suitable comeback. The Shepherd/King silenced the accusers with one very profound statement.

When those voices of condemnation and doubt from your past start taunting you, trying to distract and discourage you from full involvement in the Kingdom, take the Word, like Jesus did in the wilderness, and put them out of business.

End of Act VI, Scene 1

Act VI, Scene II
A Mature Relationship
Song of Solomon 7:1-7

1 - 7 How beautiful are thy feet with shoes, O prince's daughter! The joints of thy thighs are like jewels, the work of the hands of a cunning workman. Thy navel is like a round goblet, which wanteth not liquor: thy belly is like a heap of wheat set about with lilies. Thy two breasts are like two young roes that are twins. Thy neck is as a tower of ivory; thine eyes like the fishpools in Heshbon, by the gate of Bath-rabbim: thy nose is as the tower of Lebanon which looketh toward Damascus. Thine head upon thee is like Carmel, and the hair of thine head like purple; the king is held in the galleries. How fair and how pleasant art thou, O love, for delights. This thy stature is like to a palm tree, and thy breasts as clusters of grapes.

I am not going to discuss all these descriptions of the Believer as seen through the eyes of her Beloved. I'll leave that to someone with a lot more theological knowledge than I have. But there are some things in these verses that I'd like you to notice.

Firstly, she has her shoes on! Unlike the time when she rebuffed the Shepherd/King's urging to come exploring with Him because she'd taken off her shoes, now she has put them on, and is prepared for whatever comes next. The Believer is ready for action. As Ephesians 6:15 says, her feet are shod with the preparation of the gospel of peace.

Secondly, the joints of her thighs are not weak from lack of exercise. They are strong from walking by faith with her Beloved. She's been claiming territory for the Kingdom. Those shoes on her feet and the spiritual muscles she has developed have definitely got His approval!

Worthy of note is what the Shepherd/King said about His Beloved's eyes. He compared them to the fishpools in Heshbon, by the gate of Bath-rabbim. According to my research, Heshbon was a city about fifty miles from Jerusalem, and it is mentioned quite often in the Old Testament. Although in its history it would be ruled by various conquerors, during King Solomon's reign it was given to the Levite priests as a place where their families would be safe. Its reputation at that time was as a peaceful, protected place. In Hebrew, the name 'Heshbon' means "he who hastens to understand or build". So, to the Eastern mind, this comparison represents someone with a peaceful, understanding heart, someone with a vision for growth. The gate of Bath-rabbim refers to the deep reservoir of life-giving water from which the women of the city would draw water on a daily basis for the needs of their families. How beautiful that, because of her spiritual maturity and experience, His Beloved could be compared to a place of peace and safety, a deep reservoir of wisdom and vision from which others could draw according to their need.

Take a moment to note how His descriptions of the Bride have been taken up a notch: a **heap** of wheat, a **tower** of ivory, the **tower** of Lebanon, hair like **purple**, stature like a **palm tree**, breasts as **clusters of grapes**. There has been a lot of growth and transformation taking place since we first met the timid and bewildered new Believer when she was a young peasant girl labouring in a leased vineyard. The Shepherd/King now has great confidence in His bride. Their love does not have a whiff of infatuation in it. It is strong and mature and has grown very deep as the two of them have traveled this spiritual journey together.

End of Act VI, Scene II

Act VI, Scene III
The Bride Shows Initiative
Song of Solomon 7:10-8:5

10 I am my beloved's, and his desire is toward me.

The Believer speaks: I am my beloved's. This is a statement of fact that indicates the security she feels in this mature relationship. It's not a prideful statement because she knows beyond a shadow of doubt that everything she is and everything she has experienced is because of His love, His mercy towards her, and His amazing grace. And so she can state, with no apology, I belong to the King. His desire is toward me. I didn't have to convince Him to love me. It was He who sought me out. It was He who led me in paths of righteousness. It was He who wanted a relationship with me, even when I was completely ignorant of His character and I had no understanding of Who He was. He came looking for me. He found me resting in my house and enticed me to follow Him into the spring sunshine. It was His idea to go up to the mountain top, not mine. It was He who knocked on my door in the nighttime, because He had something special to share with me. His desire has always been toward me. He's never once looked for an opportunity to discard me, even when I miserably failed

His expectations. He doesn't watch to see if I will make a mistake so He can terminate our relationship. No, a thousand times, NO! Even when I turn my back on Him, even when I make poor choices, even when I neglect Him, even when I fall flat on my face, His desire is toward me.

Oh, how He loves you and me!

11 - 12 Come, my beloved, let us go forth into the field: let us lodge in the villages. Let us get up early; let us see if the vine flourisheth, whether the tender grape appear, and the pomegranates bud forth: there will I give thee my loves.

I find these two verses, spoken by the Bride, very moving. How easy it would be for the Believer, who has struggled through some dark times and dangerous situations, and who is now basking in the love of her Shepherd/King, to just sit back and enjoy the sweetness of His love. Who could find fault with that? Who would judge her for resting in His presence?

But the Believer isn't immature or selfish anymore. She's no longer looking for food and rest and blessings for herself like she was when we met her in the first act. She's not complacent. She has grown remarkably, and her roots have gone down deep into the soil. She understands what is important to the Gardener. She knows the beat of His heart. And so she takes His hand and leads Him away from the place of ease. She is the one taking the initiative. He's not coaxing her or pleading with her, but rather, the Believer herself says, "Let's go out to the fields. Let's go stay in the villages for a while. Let's get up early because there's no time to waste. We need to check on the vines, we need to make sure those nasty little foxes haven't nibbled away the grapes."

The mature Believer declares, I will prove my love for you, not by staying here where it's comfortable and easy, but by going out to the field. My hands might get dirty and my fingernails may get broken out in the field. It's possible that my pretty shoes will get muddy. I will prove my love to You by being willing to stay in the village, in inconvenient places. I won't demand luxury and all the creature comforts. You will know I love you because of my willingness to get up early, while others are enjoying their rest, to check on the progress of the harvest. I know that the harvest is your heartbeat, and so I will prove my love to You by matching the beat of my heart to yours. I will be the answer to your prayer request for labourers who are willing to go into the harvest. I will lift up my eyes and look on the whitened fields that are ready to harvest. Because I love you, my Shepherd/King, I will look where you look, I will see what You see.

End of Act VI Scene III

Act VI, Scene IV
Exiting the Wilderness
Song of Solomon 8:5a

> *5 a Who is this that cometh up from the wilderness, leaning upon her beloved?*

When I read this verse, it makes me want to stand up and shout!

This is a triumphant proclamation by the Bridegroom. Earlier, we saw the Believer as she stood in awe and amazement, watching the Shepherd emerge from the wilderness, transformed into the powerful King of Glory. Now the tables are turned. The Believer is not the observer this time nor is the Shepherd/King the one being presented!

Who is this that cometh up from the wilderness? It's ME! It's YOU! It's US! The Shepherd/King stands triumphantly on the stage, just before the curtain drops for the final time. His arm is outstretched toward His Bride, the faithful Believer, the survivor. She is no longer in the wilderness. She is no longer stumbling around from one situation to another, looking for a meal and a soft place to rest. She has a song of victory on her lips. She is coming out of the wilderness!

It's clear that in order to come *out* of the wilderness, the Bride has spent some time *in* the wilderness. King Solomon states that, however long she was in that lonely place, she eventually emerged victoriously.

A "wilderness experience" implies turmoil, suffering, loneliness, hardship, struggle, rejection, weakness, grief and pain. There aren't many joyful nouns or adjectives associated with a wilderness. A wilderness is a barren place where wild beasts roam. I have lived through the pain of a wilderness experience, and I know many other believers who have suffered in ways that affected them personally and very deeply. We all bear the scars of broken relationships, shattered dreams, regretted failures, painful betrayals and other "wilderness wounds."

This wilderness experience is not something new. There were many key people in the scriptures who spent time in the wilderness, wandering, struggling, seeking and alone. Abraham, Jacob, Joseph, Moses, David and Paul can all testify to "the process of the wilderness." They all came through their difficult experience to become great leaders. Time spent in the wilderness is not punishment for wrongdoing. It doesn't mean that somehow, you've gotten off the track and are out of the perfect will of God. Time spent in the wilderness is an opportunity for God to reveal your true character to you and the purpose He has for your life. Yes, you will be tested but those tests will only prove your intention to live your life fully consecrated to God.

I love what Deuteronomy 32:10 tells us about Jacob's experience, and what God's perspective was towards Jacob during that period of his life. "He found him in a desert land, and in the waste howling wilderness; he led him about, he instructed him, he kept him as the apple of his eye." It's so important for us to understand that we are never abandoned during the difficult times in our lives, when we may feel that we're struggling just to stand upright. It is in those dark moments that our Shepherd/King is leading us, instructing us, and He is keeping us right in the center of His vision. Take heart, those of you who may find yourself trying to figure out how in the world you got here…the wilderness is not your final destination. Keep going! God has His eye on you. You are never out of His sight!

The key to future success and to overcoming the trauma we've had to deal with is found in the next four words in this verse: *leaning upon her beloved*. One thing we all learn in the wilderness is that we will never make it out on our own strength. We come out limping, changed and marked like Jacob was by his intense struggle with the angel.

Yes, eventually we will shout victory. Yes, eventually we will be able show our battle scars, our wounds that have been healed. Yes, we will have gained tremendous revelation and understanding of our precious Lord and Saviour.

But through the wilderness process we have learned, beyond the shadow of any doubt, that we will never be able to stand on our own. We will only be able to walk forward into all the blessings, wonders and challenges that Jesus has prepared for His Bride as we lean on Him. He is the source of our strength. His strength will be made perfect in our weakness. Let me personalise it: I can't make it by myself. I need Jesus every day. I will never know enough scripture, I will never be spiritually mature enough, I will never have enough experience to last one day leaning on my own understanding. I MUST lean on my Beloved.

A chorus we used to sing many years ago is playing in my memory as I write these words: Oh let me walk with You, Jesus! Don't ever leave me alone. Without you I could never, no never make Heaven my home.

If you find yourself in a wilderness today, stumbling on a difficult, shadowed path, let this message comfort you. Again, I say, the wilderness experience is not final. Jesus, Your King and Shepherd will lead you through, and you will come out on the other side, much wiser, with deeper faith and trust, and you will be leaning on your Beloved.

There is some personal responsibility involved in the duration of your wilderness experience. Of course, the prime example that springs to mind is the story of the Children of Israel wandering for more than forty years in the desert after triumphantly leaving Egypt behind under Moses' leadership. Yes, they had to traverse the desert in order to arrive at the destination God had planned for them, but it certainly wasn't His intention for them to spend forty plus years there! They had the opportunity to cross the Jordan River and enter the Promised Land after Moses had sent twelve spies to investigate all the possibilities that awaited them there, leaving the wilderness behind forever. But that required a leap of faith on their part, it required trust that God would continue to be with them. Even though there'd been manna on the ground for them to gather every morning, and even though God had miraculously provided water out of a rock, the Children of Israel chose to listen to the voice of doubt that said going into the Promised Land was too difficult because of the giants and walled cities that were there. They'd become so comfortable with manna, the thought of juicy grapes, plentiful milk and sweet honey didn't tempt them enough to take the steps that would get them out of the wilderness once and for all and into the Promised Land. Because of their unbelief, those folks spent another four decades wandering around, packing and unpacking their tents, going through the same unproductive routines day after day.

We can't always blame God for the length of time we suffer during the "wilderness experience." There are situations and times that we could speed up the process if we would simply obey His voice and take the necessary step of faith towards deliverance. It's so easy to look at the difficulties and challenges ahead and convince ourselves that, even though God has given us wonderful promises, we're better off staying put right where we are, even though we feel discouraged and unfulfilled. Why did the Children of Israel think that God would abandon them once they crossed the Jordan River? He had been their Provider and their Protecter since they'd left Egypt! That doubting generation never did *come out of the wilderness*! You won't either, if you aren't willing to rise up and move forward.

I "see" two older men conferring together at the edge of the camp. One, taller and carrying a sharp sword, who is obviously the leader, is telling the other that the time is right. The other man, wiry, with muscular arms and legs, gives him a "high five" and lifts his fist in a gesture of confidence. These two elderly gentlemen are definitely leaving the wilderness behind. It can't be soon enough for them. They were ready to go forty years ago! The leader has had a word from the Lord, that it was time to take His people across the Jordan River. And how will they proceed? Well, in the words of King Solomon, they will go forward into the long-awaited Promised Land, "leaning on their beloved!"

For all of us, the future is unknown. Tomorrow and its tomorrow are mysteries that will only be revealed to us minute by minute. But here's what the Bride knows: Just like Joshua and Caleb, she will face the unknown future, its challenges, its mountains to climb, its cities to be conquered…leaning on her Beloved. The wilderness is behind her. She's not going back in that direction ever again. Instead, she is moving forward, determined to follow her Shepherd/King wherever He chooses to lead her.

End of Act VI, Scene IV

Act VI, Scene V
The Conclusion
Song of Solomon 8:5b, 11, 13-14

5b I raised thee up under the apple tree: there thy mother brought thee forth: there she brought thee forth that bare thee.

After the revelation of the Believer/Bride as she leaves the wilderness behind her, Solomon continued by reminding the Bride that it was He who had raised her up from where she was at the beginning of this saga to where she is standing now, in a fruitful and stable place. She owes Him everything! He lovingly brings her to the awareness again that her "mother", the Church, gave her an opportunity for this wonderful new birth experience. The Bride should never make the mistake of thinking it was her own strength or intelligence that had brought her to this level of maturity. She stands only by the grace of God.

11 Solomon had a vineyard at Baal-hamon; he let out the vineyard unto keepers; every one for the fruit thereof was to bring a thousand pieces of silver.

The story of the romance between the Shepherd/King and the poor but beautiful maiden has been told with great dramatic effect: how they initially fell in love and the development of their relationship from an emotional infatuation on her part to deep revelation of His character and purpose. The audience has seen a fearful Bride, they have seen an exultant Bride, they have seen her discouraged and overwhelmed by life and they have seen her finally emerging victoriously from the wilderness, leaning on her Beloved. Nothing in their love story has been glossed over or made to appear simplistic. Her struggles from time to time have been real, as have the moments of exhilaration. The audience knows that at every level of growth and maturity the Believer reached, her Lover never once abandoned her. He never put pressure on her to respond or perform. They saw Him waiting patiently in the wings of the stage when she thought He had walked away.

Almost as an afterthought, the playwright makes a simple statement that reveals to the audience that they have been told, not a sugary fairy-tale, but a true story. His story! Solomon states, I owned a vineyard. I leased that vineyard to keepers. They each paid me an annual price of a thousand pieces of silver. It was I who stood on the edge of the vineyard and observed that beautiful, sun-burned maiden, labouring under the burden of her employment. It was I who wooed her and made her my Bride. She loves me because I loved her first!

He then steps aside to allow the Bride to bring this prophetic drama to a close.

> *13 Thou that dwellest in the gardens, the companions hearken to thy voice: cause me to hear it.*

In these final two verses of Solomon's song, the Bride again stands alone on the stage as she did in the opening scene of Act I. But this confident, mature, victorious person bears no resemblance to that inexperienced, immature, infatuated young woman we met as the curtain rose for the first time.

She speaks to her Lover in a quiet, assured voice, addressing Him as "the one that dwellest in the gardens." We are reminded once again that this Shepherd/King always chooses to honour fruitful environments with His presence. His preferred habitation is a garden, where growth is an on-going process. She knows Him well. She's traveled with Him through dark caves, up steep mountains, and out to village vineyards. He has taught her many valuable lessons on these journeys. She has caught his vision and understands that He has very specific purpose for her life. And now, as she rests in blessed quietness, her one desire is simply to hear His voice. Speak to me, she says, I'm listening. My heart is ready to obey.

14 Make haste, my beloved, and be thou like to a roe or to a young hart upon the mountains of spices.

The drama called 'The Song of Solomon' draws to a close with a plea from the Bride to the King: Make haste! I am waiting for your return.

My mind's eye sees an elderly man standing alone on the Isle of Patmos. His name is John. He has been an apostle for many decades and was once identified as 'the one whom Jesus loved'. He was given the responsibility of caring for Jesus' mother after His crucifixion and His ascension. John has suffered severe persecution in his lifetime, but has also had great experiences as a messenger of the Messiah, Jesus. In the book of Revelation, John too was taken on a journey, a revelation of Jesus Christ and His Bride, the Church. He saw visions of Heaven and the awesome rewards awaiting those who obeyed the Gospel and remained faithful. He also saw visions of God's wrath being poured out on an unrepentant earth.

After recording all that he had seen and heard during this supernatural experience, John simply wrote, He which testifieth these things saith, Surely, I come quickly. Amen. Even so, come, Lord Jesus (Revelation 22:20). To the promise of the soon coming of the Lord of Lords and King of Kings, John's response was, "Please come, Lord Jesus".

Echoes of the Bride's final statement in the Song of Solomon reverberate as John expresses his feelings. She said, "Make haste, my beloved." John's statement was, "Even so, Come, Lord Jesus."

Your Bride, your Church, your Beloved, has made herself ready. The Spirit and the Bride say, Come. We are waiting and longing for your return.

This is my story. I, Georgene Rose Shalm, am the Bride. I fell in love with this wonderful Shepherd/King whose Name is Jesus. On this spiritual journey I have definitely had some moments of fear. I have had times when I thought I'd been abandoned. I have been to the mountaintop with Jesus and had His vision imprinted on my mind and heart. I have been overwhelmed sometimes. I have been wounded by rogue watchmen. I have climbed those hidden stairs, and fallen down them, too. I have basked in the sweet presence of my Heavenly Lover. I have felt the exultation of His glory. I have traveled with Him to the fields of remote villages to check on the harvest. I have put down roots in the Word that keep me stable when the winds of trouble blow in my life. I have accepted the call to "Rise up and Come Away." This is *my* story, this is *my* song.

But it's not only my story to tell. You, the reader, can put your name in the above paragraph. This is your story, too! You are loved by the Shepherd/King. You, too, were invited on this amazing life-time journey. The invitation to come away with the Shepherd/King was extended to you, too! You are one of His beloved lilies in the field. This is *your* story, this is *your* song!

The Song of Songs, which is Solomon's. It is the greatest story ever told, the story of the King of Kings who traveled to earth in a chariot of humanity and disguised Himself as a humble Shepherd. It's the story of how He fell in love with us, and how we escaped from the taskmaster of sin to become His beloved Bride. It's the story of Jesus inviting us to rise up and come away with Him, to experience the deep things of God. And finally, it's the story of the beautiful heavenly home He has prepared for us.

This is the story: I am my Beloved's and He is mine.

End of Act VI, Scene V

Made in the USA
Monee, IL
18 June 2025

19529510R20094